A History of
PSYCHOLOGY
—— IN OUTLINE ——

A History of

PSYCHOLOGY

———————— IN OUTLINE ————————

by

PATRICK J. CAPRETTA

———————— A DELTA BOOK ————————

To my parents, who sacrificed for me.
To my wife, Suzanne, and children Eve,
Nick, and Chris, who put up with me.

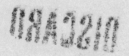

A DELTA BOOK
Published by Dell Publishing Co., Inc.
750 Third Avenue, New York, N.Y. 10017
Copyright © 1967 by Patrick J. Capretta
Delta ® TM 755118 Dell Publishing Co., Inc.
Library of Congress Catalog Card Number: 67-20523
Manufactured in the United States of America
First printing—November 1967

Contents

Preface

IN PREPARING this synopsis of the history of psychology, I had no illusions of writing a comprehensive catalogue of facts and theories. It does represent, however, an attempt at summarizing a full course of lectures that my students found useful in gaining a more thorough understanding of contemporary psychology. The outline method used in this book provides, I came to believe, not only a record of *selected* historical facts but, more importantly, a *frame of reference* by which the student can better organize the welter of information presented him.

Although much of the history included herein is based upon secondary references, the original sources were consulted whenever language and library permitted. As to writing style, I hoped to preserve, by means of paraphrase, the precision of meaning from the available literature—"dubbing in," so to speak, wherever continuity and clarity demanded.

I consider the present approach to the history of psychology to be of particular value to those students who desire an overview of the field at the start or completion of more intensive study.

I owe a considerable debt of gratitude to my students, colleagues and former professors. Of my students, I wish to thank Paul M. Bronstein, Michael N. Dietz, Andrew J. Joniak, Michael H. Kahn, and especially Sandra L. Umbenhauer for their help in rephrasing some of the more ambiguous portions of the manuscript. Their questions and comments provided a valuable source of stimulation throughout the revisions. To my colleagues James M. Hedegard and Laurence Siegel I am thankful for their many suggestions on early sections of the text. Much of my own approach to the history of psychology has been affected by the views of Harry A. Shoemaker (a former colleague at Washington State University) and the late Professor Karl F. Muenzinger, who influenced both of us. Professors Maurice P. Smith and Michael M. Wertheimer, both of the University of Colorado, have also had a hand in shaping my thoughts and encouraging my efforts toward the completion of this book. The actual manuscript would never have been completed without the kind assistance of Mrs. Cheryl R. Goeree, Mrs. Mary Kay Grimes, and the entire staff of the Instructional Research Service, Miami University. Finally, I owe much to all those individuals whose writings in and about the history of psychology made this book possible.

PATRICK J. CAPRETTA

June 1966
Oxford, Ohio

Introduction

THIS BOOK is intended to be extensive in scope. The history of psychology is traced from its early philosophical forebears, through its development within the various sciences, and finally to a stage of quasi maturity in the sophisticated systems of the late nineteenth and early twentieth centuries (with occasional glimpses into the more recent past). Coverage is also highly selective. My presentation will, I hope, give the reader a concise though *representative* view of the intellectual milieu within which the discipline developed. Instead of presenting a thorough historical chronicle, I will sketch only the more salient features in the rich evolution of psychology.

Controversy over the relative merits of the Great-Man and the Great-Times theories of the growth of a science can be circumvented, I believe, by conceiving of historical development as issuing from the indivisible amalgam of man and society. It is a truism that man both contributes to his *Zeitgeist* and is molded by it.

The body of the text is a detailed expansion of the outline appearing on pages xi-xii. Individuals are referred to by their last names except when first mentioned and for purposes of clarity. Important publication dates are given in parentheses following the author or work cited as a help in pinpointing the writer's period of literary productivity. Appendix A presents a convenient list of major contributors, their main ideas, page references to this book, and a sample of annotated bibliography for further reading. Appendix B is offered as an aid in ascertaining the relative importance of psychological concepts by means of their recurrence in history. It should be noted that this is but a single criterion by which to judge the historical value of concepts. (Other criteria might be the number of different disciplines actively entertaining the concept, and the extent and duration of interest in the concept within a particular discipline.) The glossary appearing in Appendix C is provided as a means of quick identification of the key terms (mostly in italics) used in the text.

A final word concerning the custom of some historians to judge events and ideas in retrospect. This is justifiable, I believe, if the author hopes through historical example to better place present-day conceptions in proper perspective. But the reader should realize that such evaluations are usually made on accumulated facts marshaled *after* (and maybe *because of*) the incident in question. *What appears obvious or unreasonable and silly now need not have been so then!*

I. Origins of Psychology in Philosophy: Impact of Naturalism, Rationalism, and Empiricism

> All philosophies are hypotheses, to which all
> our faculties emotional as well as logical,
> help us, and the truest of which will at the
> final integration of things be found in pos-
> session of the men whose faculties on the
> whole had the best divining power.
>
> WILLIAM JAMES

A. Primitive Animism—Preliminaries to the Study of the Mind

The belief that life and action are due to discrete, intelligent agents dwelling within the bodies of diverse objects is called *primitive animism*. Anthropological evidence indicates that it was a prevalent belief among many cultures of the past, and is still in existence in some more primitive contemporary societies.[1]

Animistic thinking as such involves no clear conception of the mind. Spirits or ghostlike entities supposedly engender whatever activity or consciousness there exists, by residing within the individual's body. The spirits, according to some versions, are presumed to wander off temporarily when the host is asleep, and they return the moment he awakens. When the host is near death, they withdraw from the mori-

[1] Excerpt from an account of a present-day Laotian military leader is a case in point: ". . . he [General Kong Le] was believed invulnerable to gunfire. The *baci*, or cotton strings, he wore tied around his wrists and a stone amulet he carried in a pouch at his waist kept his 32 souls (one for each major part of the body) from fleeing. The *phi*, or demon, who guarded him . . ."

bund body permanently. All mental and physical activities are believed to be initiated and maintained by the spirits. Not only is man inhabited by these life-giving entities, but their magic is invoked by the primitive to account for other ostensible mysteries of nature. According to this reasoning, natural phenomena as diverse as the flora and fauna, the rivers and ocean waves, wind and thunder storms are also energized by spirits. Obviously, such a belief obscures the distinction between life and nonlife. It persists in various forms throughout the world: to realize the present-day acceptance of animistic phenomena among the "more civilized" community, the reader has only to investigate some of the more occult activities of the American and British Societies for Psychical Research.

Primitive animism may arise from a confusion between the self and the external environment (*identification* and *projection*), from overgeneralization (*anthropomorphism, theriomorphism,* and *reification*), and from intense personal involvement in the affairs of others (*empathy*). Viewed in historical perspective, animistic thinking may be thought of as representing man's early attempt to comprehend the enigmas of existence. In a sense, one might say that it was propaedeutic to the scientific study of the mind (W. S. Hulin, *A Short History of Psychology,* 1934).

B. *Ionian Cosmology—Unity or Diversity in Nature*

The roots of psychology are partially embedded in the highly imaginative speculation of ancient Greek civilization. Among the initiators of philosophical thought in the Greek city-states (particularly the Ionian colonies on the western coast of Asia Minor) were the pre-Socratics, important here primarily because they provide the proper context within which to discuss the work of Socrates and his successors.

Pre-Socratic philosophers sought an elemental substance from which everything animate and inanimate in the universe might be composed. No apparent distinction was drawn between what we now understand as living and nonliving things; in fact, life was believed to be inseparable from physical matter (i.e., *hylozoism*). Some (the *monists*) sought a single substance; others (the *pluralists*) sought several. Of the monists, Thales (c. 585 B.C.) believed that water was "the mother from which all things arose and out of which they exist"; Anaximenes (c. 570 B.C.) argued for air; Anaximander (c. 580 B.C.) insisted upon the validity of a more ambiguous *apeiron* ("Boundlessness," or "the Infinite") as being the primal, indeterminate matter from which all things spring; and Heraclitus (c. 500 B.C.), emphasizing change, chose the analogy of fire, a consuming flux in which only the orderliness of the succession of things remains the same, as characteristic of all nature.[2]

Of the pluralists, Empedocles (c. 450 B.C.) claimed earth, water, air and fire to be the separate cosmic elements. In Empedocles' formulation, earth formed the solid parts of the body, water the liquids, air the vital element, and fire the rational component. Although speculation on how man perceives objects probably goes back to the beginning of human thought, Empedocles was one of the first philosophers to offer a rather convincing explanation of perception. According to the Empedoclean hypothesis that "like attracts like," the blood, which itself contains all four cosmic elements, attracts minuscular material copies of identical elements from the external world of objects. These copies, or *emanations,* then enter the blood through the body pores and conjoin with the blood elements to constitute one's perception

[2] These philosophers are noteworthy for other reasons. Thales of Miletus, for example, created a sensation by accurately forecasting a solar eclipse which occurred in 585 B.C. Anaximander advanced such ideas as the obliquity of the ecliptic, the principle of geographical mapping, and the theory that the moon shines with light from the sun. Heraclitus' views foreshadowed the modern concept of the uniformity of natural law.

of the external world. The emanation theory of perception was to hold great favor down through the ages.

Democritus' atomic theory (c. 430 B.C.) represented the first approach to cosmology which was largely devoid of hylozoism. In addition to this advance in philosophical thought, Democritus intensified speculation concerning the nature of perception by explaining it as an emanation of tiny copies of sensible things (*eidola*) which, through their impact upon the atoms of the mind, leave impressions responsible for the details of memory. He also distinguished between sensation resulting from relatively mobile atomic emanations and knowledge due to the impact of the smoothest atomic emanations. In arguing that sense experiences of warmth, taste, color, etc. exist not in the reality of atoms and the void, but only by convention, Democritus is credited by some historians as offering a very definite distinction between what later became known as *primary and secondary qualities*.

C. Greek Systematics—Development of Rationalism and Empiricism

With the shift of Greek culture from the Ionian colonies to Athens following the Persian Wars (499–478 B.C.), we find greater attention being focused on man himself as the subject of investigation. Concomitant with this concern for man grew a skeptical attitude toward the earlier cosmological dogma. Philosophers became ever more cognizant that their intellectual predecessors had speculated far beyond what was apparent through direct experience. The Sophists, a group of wandering philosopher-teachers who settled in Athens to help popularize knowledge, concluded that man's knowledge depended solely upon the individual's background of experience, thus questioning the nature of objective truth and opening the way to cosmological *nihilism* and *solipsism.* Such Sophistic thinking of Protagoras of Abdera (c. 440 B.C) and Gorgias (c. 430 B.C.) incited Socrates (c. 406 B.C.) [3] to accept the premise that the receipt of knowledge is subjective but reject the conclusion that no truth exists beyond individual opinion.

It was Plato (387 B.C.), the first of the Greek systematics, who adopted the Socratic belief and developed it in clear opposition to the beliefs of the Sophists. Plato realized the important epistemological problem involved in Sophistic thinking—must man be content with subjectivity as the sole basis for human knowledge? Extending Socratic philosophy beyond the original thought of his teacher, Plato formed the first clearly defined concept of immaterial existence. His metaphysical theory of *Ideas,* or *Forms,* imagined a realm of self-existent, immaterial, and eternal essences which constitute the divine prototypes of which all earthly objects are but imperfect and incomplete reflections. The inherent dualism in Plato's thinking is not unequivocal as a metaphysical theory, for the realm of matter is depicted as mere shadow or receptacle for the real, immutable world of forms. However, the dualistic intent is more pronounced in Plato's treatment of the psychophysical (i.e., soul-body) relationship. Here true knowledge can be contemplated only by the unifying function of the rational soul or *Psyche* (Gestalt-like conception), while the lesser parts of the soul and body [4] participate in the imperfect contributions of sensation and perception. If left to his senses alone, man could never unravel the meaning of life; it was necessary for him to apply the integrating powers of the rational soul.

[3] This date is when Socrates was made one of the Senate of Five Hundred in Athens. It is believed that Socrates wrote nothing himself; his life and teachings were recorded by Aristophanes and Xenophon, but primarily by Plato, his pupil.
[4] Concepts of the soul and mind were not clearly distinguished by Plato. Not until the early Christian philosophers Saint Paul and Saint Augustine do we find the tripartite notion of soul (in its spiritual connotations), mind, and body expressed. Plato conceived of the human soul as divisible into the rational and irrational, or more precisely, into *reason, spirit,* and *appetite.*

Concerning the psychology of perception, Plato, in supporting a kind of reverse emanation theory, suggested that man sees by spraying objects with particles shot out of the eyes. Plato is also the first major philosopher who alluded to the doctrine of *associationism* in accounting for reminiscence of ideas by *similarity* and *contiguity*.

Aristotle (340 B.C.) endeavored to put more dynamics into Platonic theory in questioning the functional relations between form and matter. Plato was concerned with *being*; Aristotle with *becoming*. His theory of causes assumed that everything is either matter or form, either potentiality or actuality. This is not to suggest that the two are separate, since form is considered by Aristotle as embedded in matter. For example, in a brass statue, brass is matter (material cause) with a multiplicity of potentialities or possibilities; the statue itself is form (formal cause), the actuality. It is the form or shape of one of the possibilities of brass. Development (efficient and final causes) is the active process by which matter becomes form and every form the matter for the next higher form. God, the prime mover, is pure actuality, the only form without matter, the only being without extension. His activity consists in pure thought, and thus in man reason represents the highest form. Aristotle also anticipated Gestalt theory in his conception of *entelechy*, the actual form or pattern which mental activity takes.

Besides the importance of Aristotle's conception of the evolution of causes, he is also to be remembered for more specific contributions, such as the distinction between sensation and perception (sensation as the motion of external objects relayed by the *pneuma* from the sense organs to the heart, and perception as the "common sense" function of the heart which synthesizes the sensory elements into units), empiricism in science, the doctrine of association (elaborating on Plato's views, suggesting *contiguity* as the fundamental law, accompanied by *similarity* and *contrast*), and the principle of *catharsis* (purging oneself of disturbing emotions by art, particularly via the tragic drama). The Sophists had promulgated extreme sensationism; Socrates and Plato had counteracted with extreme rationalism. Attempting to reconcile these two extremes, Aristotle interposed a form of empiricism which stressed experience *and* reason as prerequisites for wisdom. It is no wonder that Aristotle holds such a revered status in the annals of thought.

Following Aristotle's death (322 B.C.), the interest of Greek intellectuals turned more to ethics and morality in an attempt to check the social decay of their nation.[5] Both the Epicureans and the Stoics developed ethical theories in response to this need. Epicurus (c. 306 B.C.) modified the atomistic theory of Democritus to show that each human being is an independent agent supreme unto himself. His emanation theory of perception was similar to that of Empedocles. In relation to psychology, the main importance of the Stoics (Zeno, Cleanthes, Chrysippus—from about 308 B.C.) lies in their empiricist philosophy, agreeing with Aristotle, although specifying unequivocally that reason itself is not a product of experience. They also held that human individuality evolves from the eternal cosmic fire (accepting Heraclitus' cosmological notion) and is therefore itself eternal. This might well be the first definite statement, in the history of thought, of the individual human soul.

D. *Alexandrian Science—Advancement in the Biological Sciences*

In Egypt, the city of Alexandria with its great museums and libraries became not only the center of mathematical studies in the East, but also a haven for the sciences created

---

[5] This change of interest was due partly to the decline of Greek political power after the death of Alexander the Great (323 B.C.). Civil strife and the encroachment of Roman imperialism accentuated the problem of human welfare.

by Aristotle.[6] Herophilus (c. 300 B.C.) and his younger contemporary, Erasistratus, made significant discoveries in both anatomy and physiology. They were among the first to perform experiments *in vivo* identifying many important parts of the nervous system. Among their more important contributions were the distinction between the cerebrum and the cerebellum, the description of the optic nerve and parts of the eye, the description of nerves as hollow tubes through which pass animal spirits manufactured in the brain, the suggestion that different nerves (conceived of as ramifications of arteries) mediate sensory-motor activities, and the emphasis on the greater anatomical complexity of man's cerebral cortex as compared with that of infrahuman animals.

E. *Early Christian Period—The Analysis of Consciousness*

Efforts to establish ethics upon a basis of reason had failed because many of the apparent contradictions in life could not be resolved by existing knowledge. Reason alone was discredited, and philosophy to a large extent became the handmaiden of theology in turning to the supernatural for guidance. To this was added cultural plunder from the Roman invasions in Asia and Africa in the form of Oriental mysticism.

Preceding Christian thought, Philo of Alexandria (c. 30 A.D.) attempted to join Hebrew theism with Greek rationalism. As a result, life was conceived of as the restoration of the fallen soul—a regeneration, as it were, through the attainment of wisdom. Philo also alluded to a distinction between concepts of the soul and mind, which was developed

[6] The ruling Ptolemies of Egypt made Alexandria a cultural capital by establishing there the greatest library of the ancient world. This splendid collection included more than a half million rolls of papyrus (a kind of paper made from reeds), the equivalent of tens of thousands of books today.

more thoroughly in the thinking of the early Christians Saint
Paul and Saint Augustine of Hippo.

Saint Paul (67 A.D.) trichotomized human life into soul
(or *pneuma*), which, being immortal, nurtures on faith and
virtue; mind (or *psyche*), with which man reasons; and
body, the avenue of all sensation. Interest in knowing how
the mind becomes aware of the existence of the soul led to
a psychological examination of the nature of mind as revealed through the analysis of consciousness.

Saint Augustine (395 A.D.), in his discourse on consciousness, was one of the first persons to explicitly adopt introspection as a definite method of psychological investigation.
Consciousness for Saint Augustine represented the most certain event in one's experience, because even the act of
doubting consciousness asserts its very existence (see Descartes, p. 18). Another important Augustinian contribution
concerns the unifying nature of consciousness. Conceived of
in this manner, consciousness serves to actively combine isolated stimuli into whole units, as in the experience of subjective rhythm by which uniform successions of sounds are
marked off into groups (similar to Aristotle's conception of
the "common sense," and an important aspect of later Gestalt
theory).

F. Scholastic Period—Doctrine of Twofold Truth

Centuries of great population shifts coupled with the profound asceticism of the Church (due primarily to the painful
early years of Christianity) deterred many European scholars
from contemplations of physical nature to serious attempts
at rationalizing their religious faith. Though endeavors of
this sort were generally logical in nature, they were many
times devoid of verifiable content. A few specific cases serve
to illustrate the kinds of contradictory conclusions which
may arise from deductive discourse alone: Saint Anselm of

Canterbury (c. 1080) claimed that ideas arise only if there is an objective reality to cause them, and therefore, for example, the idea of perfection proves the existence of a perfect Being (*realism*); Berengar (c. 1045) and Roscellinus (c. 1100), on the other hand, maintained that general ideas exist only as labels or names in human thinking and are the products of the experience of physical particulars which are in themselves the sole reality (*nominalism*). As an attempt at compromise, Abélard (c. 1120) advanced the theory of *conceptualism*, which stated that widely held ideas or concepts are less than ultimate realities, yet more than mere names.

It is an interesting historical fact that for a long time Aristotelian science was largely a monopoly of Arabic scholars, who had access to the libraries where most of Aristotle's works were held.[7] The early Christians were in possession of Plato's philosophical writings, but little of Aristotelian philosophy, with the exception of his work on logic, was available to enrich their thought. By the time of St. Thomas Aquinas (c. 1260), however, much of Aristotle's writings had become available in western Europe. The great Greek philosopher's work became so influential that it threatened to surpass the authority of Church dogma. It was the extremely prolific Aquinas,[8] who furnished the means of protecting both su-

---

[7] The Islamic dynasty grew rapidly due to military conquests during the seventh and eighth centuries. Syria and Persia were conquered almost simultaneously by two armies. Between 646 and 650, the Arabs added Egypt, the major Byzantine naval base and possessor of Greek literature. The Moslems came to share with the Byzantines the role of preserver and modifier of the classical works of philosophy and science through the efforts of such men as the great Spanish Moslem Averroës (c. 1160), whose commentaries on Aristotle translated from Arabic into Latin were available to the Christian West before the original Greek text of Aristotle himself. (C. Brinton, J. B. Christopher, and R. L. Wolff, *A History of Civilization*, 1955.)

[8] Aquinas wrote voluminously in philosophy and theology. His *Summa contra Gentiles* by itself is 60,000 words longer than the whole of Berkeley's philosophical writings. Commentaries on Aristotle in the gigantic *Summa theologica*, which Aquinas left unfinished at his death, fill some sixty volumes. In light of this proliferation, it is interesting that in the Middle Ages

premacy for religion and security for the sciences in his *Doctrine of Twofold Truth* (religious truth based on clerical authority and scientific truth founded on empiricism).

Of a more specific nature, Aquinas modified Saint Paul's distinction between mind and soul in conceiving of the latter as *form* in the Aristotelian sense. That is to say, although soul remains immortal, it becomes "individualized" through its contact with a particular body and mind.

Aquinas did not command, outside the Dominican Order, any unique authority among the Scholastics. The reformationists despised him as a logic-chopper, a half-Christian Aristotelian who exalted reason to the detriment of faith.

II. Evolution of Psychology in the Natural Sciences: Man as a Part of Nature

> *The mathematical ideal of science does not imply that nature is somehow committed to fitting the specific patterns that have proved fruitful, so far, in this or that part of science. Ambitious programs for making biology or sociology or psychology mathematical—that is, physics-like—leave a painful impression that one is giving orders to nature. But the mathematical ideal is tenable, and not because of any secret knowledge that nature is strait-jacketed by a particular set of cherished patterns. It is not the confinement of nature, but the plenitude of mathematics, that makes the ideal tenable. And only a small part of that plenitude is yet reduced to orderly development.**
>
> DAVID HAWKINS

A. Major Developments in Astronomy and Physics and Their Effects on Psychology

With the fall of feudalism and the dissemination of the Near East culture, man was again made cognizant of the importance of understanding his natural surroundings. The Renaissance began in the latter part of the fourteenth century and reached its zenith in the sixteenth century. Humanism made great strides forward during this period, in the efforts of men such as Machiavelli (1515), Pomponazzi (1517), Luther (1517) and Vives (1538). They endeavored to revive interest in the biopsychological as well as the

* From *The Language of Nature*. Freeman, 1965. By courtesy of the publisher.

sociological study of man, which had been severely curtailed during the logic-splitting period of Scholasticism. Of particular importance to the history of psychology were the developments in astronomy that gave rise to a reinterpretation of man's relationship to his universe.

1. *Copernican revolution*. In 1543, Nicolaus Copernicus, a Polish astronomer, proposed a hypothesis which conflicted with the prevailing Ptolemaic system of astronomy.[1] Although his heliocentric view was, as a concept, simpler (though not in its mechanics) than the geocentric theory of the Alexandrian astronomer Ptolemy, it had serious philosophical and practical implications. For example, Copernican theory was incompatible with the traditional interpretation of the Bible, with the physics of Aristotle, and with common-sense knowledge that the earth was in fact standing still. Its acceptance would mean discarding the laws of motion that had been accepted as self-evident since the days of Aristotle and looking for radically new ones. The considerable resistance to the seeming unnaturalness of the proposed heliocentric system was allayed somewhat in the discoveries of Brahe (1575), Kepler (1609), and Galileo (1632). With Brahe's careful observations on the motions of heavenly bodies, Kepler's ingenious mathematical formulations of planetary orbits, and Galileo's stalwart defense of Copernican theory recorded in his *Dialogo* (for additional material see A. D. White's *A History of the Warfare of Science with Theology in Christendom*, 1955),[2] the intellectual world

[1] Actually Copernicus' hypothesis was published posthumously (or more precisely while he was on his deathbed) by Osiander who presumably wrote a grovelling preface suggesting that the new astronomy was simply a hypothesis and not to be construed as fact. It should be noted that a third century B.C. astronomer, Aristarchus, under the patronage of the Ptolemies of Egypt, advanced the following hypothesis: The fixed stars and the sun remain unmoved, but the earth revolves about the sun in the circumference of a circle, the sun lying in the middle of the orbit. Some three centuries earlier, Pythagoras, and after him Philolaus, suggested that the earth and planets moved about a central fire.

[2] The Inquisition at Rome decided unanimously against Galileo's defense of the heliocentric theory as follows: "The first proposition, that the sun is the center and does not revolve about the earth, is foolish, absurd, false in

took notice. It is curious that even Brahe, who made observations contradictory to Ptolemaic astronomy, was not a radical theorist. Refusing to accept Copernicus' heliostatic hypothesis, he proposed a system in which the earth was at rest in the center of the universe, and the sun went around it, carrying all the planets. As might be expected, it was considered to be a sound conservative theory by the Church authorities.

Along with the acceptance of the mathematical truth of the Copernican system grew the forbidding philosophical realization that man was no longer supreme in the universe but rather a hapless inhabitant of one of the many planets which orbited the sun. Relegation of man to a peripheral status in the scheme of things represented a sharp and philosophically significant break from Aristotelian anthropocentrism.

2. *Galilean metaphysics.* Galileo's mathematical metaphysics (for further coverage see E. A. Burtt's *Metaphysical Foundations of Modern Physical Science,* 1924) led him, like Kepler, to the doctrine of *primary* and *secondary qualities,* only with the Italian the distinction was more fully developed and explicitly stated.[3] Galileo distinguished clearly between that in the world which is absolute, objective, immutable, and mathematical (primary qualities) and that which is relative, subjective, fluctuating, and sensible (secondary qualities). The latter were declared to be the effects on the senses of the primary qualities which are themselves "real" in nature. This distinction in forms of reality marks a significant dichotomy between man and physical nature. It

---

theology, and heretical, because expressly contrary to Holy Scripture"; and "the second proposition, that the earth is not the center but revolves about the sun, is absurd, false in philosophy, and, from a theological point of view at least, opposed to the true faith."

[3] In Kepler's version there was no clear statement of the subjectivity of secondary qualities. He apparently conceived of them as out "there" in the astronomical world, like the primary qualities, with the exception that they were not so real or so basic. It should be recalled that Democritus, some two thousand years before, had alluded to such a distinction.

seems inevitable that under these circumstances man should appear to be outside the real world, for was he not merely a bundle of secondary qualities! Refutation of Aristotle's anthropocentric view was underscored by the Galilean perspective of man as an inconsequential spectator in the real world of mathematics. (Note the relationship between this view and the ancient Pythagorean attempt to explain all things in and of the universe in the abstract language of mathematics, i.e., number or geometrical form.) [4]

Some of the more unpleasant implications of such a cold look at man's earthly status is eloquently spelled out in the following quotation from *African Genesis* (Delta Books, 1963), a fascinating book on the evolution of man by Robert Ardrey:

> . . . should a man ever attain a state of total maturity—ever come to see himself, in other words, in perfect mathematical relationship to the two and one-half billion members of his species, and that species in perfect mathematical relationship to the tide of tumultuous life which has risen upon the earth and in which we represent but a single swell; and furthermore come to see our earth as but one opportunity for life among uncounted millions in our galaxy alone, and our galaxy as but one statistical improbability, nothing more, in the silent mathematics of all things—should a man, in sum, ever achieve the final, total, truthful Disillusionment of Central Position, then in all likelihood he would no longer keep going but would simply lie down, wherever he happened to be, and with a long-drawn sigh return to the oblivion from which he came.

3. *Newtonian mathematics.* The work of Sir Isaac Newton

[4] Kurt Lewin (*Principles of Topological Psychology*, 1936), in describing Galileo's revolt against Aristotle, distinguishes three epochs in the evolution of psychology. At first came the Aristotelian, or "speculative," stage in which philosophers attempted to discover the essence of things and the final cause behind all phenomena. In the second stage, "descriptive" in nature, psychologists in reaction against far-fetched speculation concentrated on the collection and careful description of facts. Finally in the 1930's, Lewin felt it was time for the third epoch, the Galilean, or "constructive," in which the goal was the discovery of laws and the prediction of individual cases.

(1687) represents the greatest combination of mathematical and empirical methods in the seventeenth century. His genius inspired Alexander Pope's well-known couplet: "Nature and Nature's laws lay hid in night; God said, 'Let Newton be,' and all was light." Newton's contribution consisted both in the development of new mathematical methods and in the extension of Kepler's laws.[5] He employed the empirical data of other scientists as well as his own in the formulation of physical laws of great generality; for example, his mathematics revealed the homogeneity of gravitational forces contained within the solar system. It was conceivable that generalizations of the same breadth and precision could be had in the biological sciences.

Of more psychological interest, Newton is credited with the first physical analysis of spectral colors (*A New Theory about Light and Colours*, 1672, and *Opticks*, 1704) in demonstrating that a prism separates white sunlight into the pure spectral colors, which can in turn be recombined into white light. He also demonstrated that every primary color has a complementary color, which, when mixed together, gives white light. Of no mean importance was Newton's assertion that light rays in-and-of-themselves are not "coloured" but become so as a result of the action of light on the retina. It is also interesting to note that Newton favored a corpuscular theory of light (i.e., a stream of minute corpuscles which fly through space), whereas Christian Huygens (1690), the great Dutch mathematician and astronomer, maintained that light consists of vibrations or waves of luminiferous ether.

---

[5] Johannes Kepler, a German astronomer, deduced three laws of planetary motion from data obtained by his Danish teacher, Tycho Brahe.

a. The orbits of all planets are ellipses with the sun located in one of the two foci.

b. The motion of planets along their elliptical orbits proceeds in such a way that an imaginary line connecting the sun with the planet sweeps over equal areas of the planetary orbit in equal intervals of time.

c. (Published nine years later.) The square of periods of revolution of different planets stand in the same ratio as the cubes of their mean distances from the sun.

For more on these laws, see George Gamow, *Gravity* (1962).

Both theories were found valuable in accounting for the relevant facts. Experimentally, light is emitted and absorbed as if it were a stream of particles, but it travels past obstacles as if it were a wave motion. The wave-particle duality appears to be an unsolved dilemma of modern physics.

B. *Baconian Empiricism—Establishment of a Method of Inquiry*

Francis Bacon (1620) strove to develop a secular philosophy, one unencumbered by religious qualifications. Inspired by the Renaissance, and in revolt against Scholastic logic, the English philosopher proposed an inductive method of discovering truth, founded upon empirical observation, analysis of data, inferred hypotheses, and verification of hypotheses through repeated observation and experiment. He sharpened the appreciation for the scientific attitude by describing some of the impediments or prejudices which may hinder the inductive search for facts. The prejudices, which Bacon called *Idols* or false models of conduct, include: idols of the cave (personal bias), tribe (allegiance to racial dogma), market place (failure to define terms adequately), and theater (blind acceptance of tradition and authority). Bacon insisted that inductive inquiry must be a cautious, laborious, step-by-step process. The results of such inquiry can never be more than provisional because of the possibility of undiscovered negative instances.[6]

Of a more specific nature, Bacon outlined several programs for the objective study of man, including a statistical survey of man's intellectual and physical abilities, examination of human facial expressions, a compendium of dreams, and an investigation of racial customs.

[6] To a certain extent, B. F. Skinner's admonition to psychologists to be wary of premature theory is akin to this position. (A highly readable reference for those interested in Bacon is Catherine Drinker Bowen's *Francis Bacon: The Temper of a Man*, 1963.)

C. Cartesian Thought—Reformulation and Sharpening of the Mind-Body Problem

René Descartes (1641) exerted a tremendous influence on developments in the fields of philosophy and science.[7] The Frenchman was an intellectual genius whose scholarly contributions extended from philosophical speculation and pure mathematics to the physiology of the animal body.

Descartes *qua* philosopher is regarded by some historians as one of the founders of modern epistemology. Dissatisfied with the lack of agreement among philosophers, he saw the need for a new philosophical method—a method as rigorous as mathematics itself. He began by questioning everything which failed to pass the test of his criterion of truth—the *clearness and distinctness* of ideas. It was his intention to submit every thought to test, every thought to doubt. Reasoned Descartes: though I might doubt everything, I cannot reasonably doubt that I, the thinking doubter, exist as a *res cogitans* (thinking substance). And thus evolved the famous Cartesian aphorism: *Cogito, ergo sum* (I think, therefore I am). This Descartes offered as an immediate intuition of his own thinking mind.

Another reality, whose existence Descartes sought to establish on various logical proofs, was God. The so-called proofs were actually superfluous, reasoned Descartes, because of the clear and distinct manner in which the idea of a Divine Existence pervades man's thoughts. No clear and distinct ideas were invariably found for an extra-mental, corporeal world; he suspected its existence, but insisted upon logical demonstration as essential to establish this as well as

[7] Descartes' extraordinary influence on subsequent thought was probably due in part to the fact that he was one of the first major philosophers since Boethius (c. 500) to write for intelligent amateurs and gentlemen. It was common practice among other philosophers to couch their scholarly discussions within a specialized and esoteric framework of concepts.

other supposed truths. By arguing that God would be a deceiver had He allowed men to think that bodies exist if they really do not, Descartes convinced himself that bodies also exist by virtue of their very presence in the mind.[8] (As inevitable certainties of the mind, God and the self—in addition to geometrical axioms and conceptions of space, time, and motion—were considered by Descartes to be *innate ideas*.) Descartes did admit that people often make mistakes in perception; this was due not to a weakness in God's ways, but to a lack of restraint in judgment, for which man himself is to blame.

Satisfied with the logical fundamentals of his philosophy, Descartes proceeded to expand on the inherent dualism of his system by postulating two distinct classes of reality: a class of material things (*res extensa*) and a class of immaterial things (*res inextensa*) characterized by mental and spiritual qualities only. The mind, evidenced in thought, is studied introspectively; while the body, characterized in action, is studied by scientific methods. The relation between the body and the mind in humans was in terms of their *interaction*, the pineal gland being the point at which the two discrete realities interacted. The soul could, at will, sway the gland from side to side, thus opening or closing the pores in the brain. By this means, the animal spirits, stored in the cerebral ventricles, flowed down the tiny "tubes," or motor nerves, to the muscles, filling and swelling them. The animal spirits could also be liberated by means of involuntary sensory nerve activity (i.e., reflex action), whereby the tubes leading to the pineal gland would activate it much as the soul could on a voluntary basis.

But the basic dilemma, the age-old bone of contention among the mind-body theorists, persisted: Could an incorporeal reality affect a corporeal substance? Or, as put by

[8] An interesting similarity is seen between Cartesian and empiricist thought, especially concerning the reliance on God to substantiate the true existence of the world. With God as referent, Descartes accepted the world of objects, while Berkeley conceded only the existence of minds.

Descartes's leading opponent, French atomist Pierre Gassendi (1641): "How may the union of the corporeal with the incorporeal be conceived?" Attempts to solve this enigma have been many and varied. A list of the suggested logical solutions to the mind-body problem and major proponents include: (a) *Materialistic Monism*—processes of the mind are in fact physiological processes (Thomas Hobbes); (b) *Idealistic Monism*—all the so-called physical processes, including physiological ones, are in fact of the same kind as the processes of the mind (George Berkeley); (c) *Psychophysical Parallelism*—there are two distinct realities which do not interact but function in parallel fashion much as two clocks running at the same speed and showing the same time (Gustav Fechner); (d) *Epiphenomenalism*—the mind is a by-product of nervous processes, although belonging to a different basic reality (Thomas Huxley); (e) *Double-Aspect* —there are two distinct entities that are dependent upon a third fundamental reality of an unclear nature for their integrated relationship; [9] (f) *Double-Language*—the processes of the mind and body are basically the same, but we talk about each one by means of a different vocabulary (most modern-day psychologists).

This list of logical solutions was adapted from Karl Muenzinger's *Psychology: The Science of Behavior* (1942). Needless to s⬛⬛the tenability or untenability of any of these logical solutions depends upon certain *a priori* assumptions. There is no *a posteriori* way of deciding in favor of one over the others. Any rigorous experimentalist, as Muenzinger contends, formulates the mind-body problem in terms of physiology and overt behavior as two sets of observed events to be correlated. In this way it does not demand a "solution" but a resolute experimental attack.

[9] This solution of the mind-body problem is essentially the *occasionalism* of Arnold Geulincx (1655), except for the specific suggestion that it is God who "on occasion" coordinates physical fact with mental activity.

III. Reaction to Cartesian Rationalism: Struggle with the Problem of Knowledge

> Des Cartes *maintained that thought was the essence of the mind; not this thought or that thought, but thought in general. This seems to be absolutely unintelligible, since everything, that exists, is particular. And therefore it must be our several particular perceptions, that compose the mind.*
>
> DAVID HUME

A. *British Empiricism—Early Theories of Perception, Learning, and Memory*

The rationalist insisted that man had the innate capacity of becoming directly aware of mental and physical substance, just as the medieval realist [1] had maintained that man could become cognizant of universals. I have emphasized Descartes' confidence in his clear and distinct ideas concerning the material world. Other philosophers, however, came gradually to insist that man could experience physical substance and causal law indirectly and, on occasion, by inference only. They repudiated the Cartesian belief that clear and distinct ideas guarantee their own validity. What was needed was critical self-inspection and analysis of the content of experience, with particular stress on the origin and development of ideas. This psycho-philosophical analysis was attempted from three points of view. In France and Germany

[1] Medieval realism produced at times a caricature of Plato's theory of Ideas. Some of the followers of Saint Augustine outdid Plato in their fervor to make the Universal, or Form, the prominent reality in the universe. According to this view, *Universals* are the only true realities—the *Particular* is simply the intersection of several Universals (Erigena, c. 848.).

there developed a modified form of rationalism which consisted of a logical disquisition on the modes of activity, or *faculties*, by which the mind functions. Also in France there was a continuation of the naturalism which had resulted from the mechanistic aspects of Cartesian theory. And finally, in England the inquiry was founded upon empiricism, which involved an attempt to trace the origin of ideas to actual experience and to disclose the laws which underlie the organization of these elements of the mind. It is with this last development that I will begin.

Although Locke is usually thought of as introducing British empiricism, I choose to start with the English social philosopher Thomas Hobbes (1650), who also considered knowledge empirical in origin. He reacted even more emphatically than Descartes to the psychological implications revealed in the scientific discoveries of his age. Hobbes regarded matter and motion as the least common denominators of all man's percepts, and bodies and their movements as the only subject matter of philosophy. Consciousness, considered from the viewpoint of sensation and cognition, was a jarring of the nervous system, and in its affectional and volitional aspects a nervous reaction to the jar. This complete materialistic empiricism (reminiscent of Democritus' atomic theory) fostered the belief that man does not know the external world directly but only by inference based upon the motions within himself.

John Locke (1690) is considered to be the first great British empiricist who declared that there were no innate ideas and that all man's knowledge of the world comes from the senses. For Locke the mind at birth is a *tabula rasa,* except for the few inchoate impressions formed during prenatal existence. Thus, even the most abstract ideas, such as power, infinity, identity, and substance, arise from experience. Evidence for this assumption, Locke maintained, is based upon the facts that children are totally unaware of the most universally accepted axioms, and that racial groups differ radically in their beliefs. In addition, he supported the remarkably prophetic idea (first put forward by Molyneux in a letter to Locke, 1690) that the investigation of rare cases of adult recovery of sight following congenital blindness would shed light on the development of human perception.[2]

Locke considered two elemental kinds of experience: *ideas of sensation* and *ideas of reflection,* either of which may be simple or complex. The former arise in the separate senses and indicate the existence of an external physical world, while ideas of reflection arise from the "perception of the operations of our own minds within us." Furthermore, the occurrence of reflective thought implies the presence of a spiritual soul, presumably the essence of life with which man is born.

Galileo's distinction between primary and secondary qualities was given further consideration by Locke. Primary qualities—or extension, figure, motion, rest, solidity, and number—produce in man ideas resembling the physical world which excites them; whereas the secondary qualities are "nothing in the objects themselves, but powers to produce various sensations in us by their primary qualities" (e.g., taste, color, sound, smell). The subjective nature of the latter phenomena is demonstrated by chilling one hand and heating the other, then placing both hands together in a pan of water of neutral temperature, noting that the heated hand feels cool and the chilled one warm (Locke's well-known demonstration of temperature contrast).

Locke's thinking led him to the notion of associationism, conceiving of complex ideas as the combination of simple

[2] But it was M. V. von Senden who actually reported cases of this kind as late as 1932. However, more recent investigations show that the lack of veridical perception following blindness could be due to many factors, including loss of critical periods for maturation, continued reliance upon the previously available senses, and associated emotional disturbances. In short, it is misleading to speculate concerning normal perceptual development on the basis of these cases of arrested vision, for, as some investigators have argued, adults who have their sight restored are not living fossils of normal infants.

ones. While the association of ideas (a phrase coined by Locke) or, rather, combination of simple ideas was discussed to some extent in terms of "pleasure," "natural correspondence," "chance," and "custom," definite establishment of the doctrine is credited to later writers.

The Irish philosopher George Berkeley (1710), although agreeing with Locke's empiricism, did not accept the Lockian argument that the material world is the necessary cause of man's ideas. Instead, he denied the existence of an independent world of bodies by arguing that their existence consists solely in perceptibility, "*esse* is *percipi*." Berkeley also asserted that the source of all ideas was a universal mind (God), and it is only through the virtue of such divine perception that a real world of things exists. By means of this "outside," albeit supernatural, referent for man's experiences, Berkeley was barely able to rescue his system from the inevitable trap of solipsism.

Although his epistemological position is of great importance, Berkeley's renown in the history of psychology is due more to his theory of visual space perception, which many historians consider to be the first wholly pertinent treatment of a psychological problem. Rejecting Descartes's appeal to "natural geometry" (geometry of optics) as an explanation of depth perception, Berkeley maintained that the perception of space results from experiences developed in the early years by touching and handling objects giving rise to ideas of magnitude (movements over surfaces) and distance (movements to and fro).[3] From the continued connection with touch the visual sensations become associated with object positions in space. This is the essence of the empirical theory of space perception.

David Hume (1740), the Scottish historian and philoso-

[3] Although it is clear that Berkeley (and even Descartes) was writing about *kinesthetic* cues, we have to wait upon Sir Charles Bell (*On the Nervous Circle Which Connects the Voluntary Muscles with the Brain*, 1826) and even Charles S. Sherrington (1906), the English physiologist, for a more explicit account of this phenomenon of proprioception.

pher, brought empiricism to its logical resting place, a dead end, as it were, leaving the world scheme of Descartes and Locke a mere flux of discrete impressions and ideas (conceived of as faint copies of impressions) which combine and recombine into pattern after pattern. Concepts, including those of the self, were conceived as discrete ideas strung together according to the principles of associationism of which there are three for Hume—*resemblance* ("a picture naturally makes us think of the man it was drawn for"); *contiguity* ("when St. Denis is mentioned, the idea of *Paris* naturally occurs"); and *causation* ("when we think of the son, we are apt to carry our attention to the father"). The external world, too, is nothing more than a system of correlated impressions following one upon the other to produce the illusion of causal necessity—i.e., *cause is correlation*. Epistemological analysis of the Humean variety reduces these impressions to discrete events, like the film strip stopped and viewed exposure by exposure. As with other great philosophers, Hume had a varied effect on his successors. Reid and Kant opposed his skepticism and subjectivism, while Mach and Pearson favored his positivism.[4] In a more practical sense, Hume (like Locke) was an active diplomatist, being for a time a greatly admired and flattered chargé d'affaires at the British Embassy in Paris.

David Hartley (1749), the English physician, furnished a quasi-physiological basis for the doctrine of associationism. Taking over Newton's conjecture of a vibratory action in the optic nerves, Hartley maintained that vibrations occur in the white medullary substance of the nerves which parallel sensations or conscious events. The diminutive vibrations (*vibratiuncles*) resulting from subsiding nervous activity in the head are paralleled by ideas or memory images (a form

[4] Hume provided the groundwork for a new school of Empiricism known as the *Logical Positivists*. They took over Humean skepticism in arguing that no statement which cannot be tested or verified by empirical observation can be considered meaningful. This philosophic position is considered in more detail later in this book.

of psychophysical parallelism following in the footsteps of Humean philosophy). Vibrations also continue to the muscles, and when they subside (being somewhat self-perpetuating) they leave a disposition for motor vibratiuncles. Hartley, unlike Hume, made contiguity and repetition the sole laws of both simultaneous (or synchronous) and successive association. If sensations (vibrations) A, B, C occur together often enough, then a reoccurrence of sensation A may arouse ideas (vibratiuncles or miniature vibrations) B and/or C, or the appropriate muscular movements.[5] The detailed and lucid manner in which Hartley enunciated his theory accounts for the title usually given to him, "founder of the associationist school in psychology." [6]

B. *Scottish Psychology—Appeal to Common Sense*

The conditions that prevailed in Scotland, where religious and political beliefs were antithetical to the skepticism inherent in the empiricist philosophy, served to set in bold relief the extremes to which careful and diligent analytic thought had taken man. Thomas Reid (1764), who originated the Scottish or so-called Common Sense School, reacted strongly against the idealism of Berkeley and the skeptical empiricism of Hume. Reid's most salient point was evident in his doctrine of *common sense*, hypothesizing a natural instinct by virtue of which man accepts certain fundamental principles as postulates without requiring rea-

[5] This appears, in a general way, to be the sensory counterpart of the concept of *redintegration* (actually credited to the Scottish psychologist Sir William Hamilton, 1836), which is defined as the tendency, when a response has been made to a complex stimulus, for that same response later to be made to any part of the stimulus complex. Hamilton's conception is less restricted than Hartley's in that it accounts for the recall of the whole situation as a unit rather than a prearranged series as suggested by the orthodox associationists.
[6] The work of Reverend John Gay, *Dissertation Concerning the Fundamental Principle of Virtue or Morality* (1731), influenced Hartley in his general application of associationism.

sons for their truth. Consciousness common to mankind, Reid contended, has too great an "immediacy" to be dependent upon physiological processes, and so must come from God.

Of a more specific nature, Reid and his chief Scottish disciple, Dugald Stewart, are important also for their contributions to the development of *faculty psychology*. A discussion of faculty psychology can be justifiably included under a number of different headings, e.g., with the Scholastics, with the German rationalist Christian Wolff (1734), and with Gall and the phrenologists. But it should be noted that Reid and his colleague did speak of faculties as the capacity of the soul to carry out in a unified manner certain psychological activities. In a sense, then, faculty psychology viewed in this way suggests a "double enumeration" (present-day historian Gardner Murphy's term) of all mental processes, so that the specific process of, say, memory is backed up by the integrated power or faculty for memory.

Although Thomas Brown (1820) represents three schools of thought (English, French, and Scottish), his major tie to the Scottish movement lies in his acceptance of the cardinal doctrine that the mind is not a mosaic of ideas but a unity of faculties. Nevertheless, needing some principle to help account for the work of the mind, he borrowed heavily from the associationists in distinguishing between primary and secondary laws of association, or "suggestion" (Berkeley's term), as he preferred to call it. According to Brown, suggestion is based on the three primary laws of *resemblance, contrast,* and *contiguity in time and place* (all subsumed under the general principle of "coexistence"). In addition, Brown offered nine secondary laws which serve to modulate the action of the primary laws. These modern-sounding laws can be summarized as follows: (a) *duration, liveliness, frequency,* and *recency* of the original sensations; (b) a type of redintegration based upon *fewer alternative associations* (i.e., something associated with one person can scarcely be experienced without recalling that person to mind); (c) other conditions having to do with the effects of constitutional differences, emotions, temporary states of the body, and habits upon the development of suggestions. Thus it is apparent that Brown, while avoiding the term *association,* advanced *associationism.* Nineteenth-century associationism would have been considerably more viable had it taken more of Brown's suggestions seriously.

Brown also developed an explanation of space perception similar to Berkeley's empirical theory. He assumed that there is an elementary "feeling of succession or time," which is aroused during muscular activity. This combination of time and muscle senses in an associative manner produces the perception of space.

C. *Early German Psychology—Rapprochement between Rationalism and Empiricism*

One of Immanuel Kant's main contributions (1781) to psychology is probably his insistence that the process of perception be conceived of as a unitary act. The great German philosopher questioned, in a more fundamental sense than did the advocates of the Scottish school, the very core of classical associationism. According to the environmentally oriented associationists, the mind was a mosaic of independent elements having little more than an empirical "adhesive" binding them together. The rationalists, on the other hand, conceived of the mind as a ready-made, self-contained entity capable of a spontaneous and intuitive apprehension of the real world. Kant sought to rectify the impractical features of both rationalism and empiricism, taming one and developing the other. This led him to an appraisal of consciousness itself, conceiving of its basic characteristic as *synthesis*—that is, its function of combining a multitude of diverse sensations into a meaningful unity. The principal means by which this synthesis occurs is through the *pure intuitions* of *time* and *space*. This is so, argued Kant, because it is inconceivable to imagine anything not occurring in time and/or space. When various discrete sensations group themselves about an object in time and space, there results not a mere conglomeration of unrelated stimuli, but a meaningful perception. Kant also introduced *a priori categories* (i.e., logical constructs of the mind prior to the phenomena which must necessarily conform to these categories) to explain how perceptions become arranged about the ideas of cause, unity, necessity, etc., to form conceptions. In this sense the categories or "pure principles of the understanding" serve to mold and classify perceptions into the ordered concepts of thought. Thus, sensations are not organized, as the extreme empiricist believed, solely by the world in itself, but by the very nature of man's mind.

Regarding psychology proper, Kant divided its subject matter into epistemology and anthropology. He declared that the events of the mind occur in a "flux of time" and so could not be reduced to a timeless order (i.e., mathematical), thus discouraging laboratory study of these phenomena. So proscribed, Herbart, Fechner, and others were incited to contest such an important edict.

D. *French Materialism and Naturalism— Man as a Machine*

Seventeenth-century France was unaware of much of the philosophical and scientific work in England. This was largely due to the disdain with which the French monarchy looked upon their anarchistic and rebellious northerners. It was Voltaire's visit to England (1726–28) that brought the dissemination of Locke and Berkeley's empiricism, and Newton's physics. Many of his enlightening translations appeared in the radical publications of the French Encyclopedists.

Julien Offray de La Mettrie (1747), another of the contributors to the *Encyclopédie*, featured man as entirely a machine, thus exaggerating one aspect of Cartesian dualism. Conceiving of the soul as a product of bodily growth, La Mettrie argued that mental states could be depicted in the same mechanistic manner as any other palpable reality. La Mettrie took Locke's empiricism as corroborating proof that knowledge, the content of the brain, is limited to bodily activities; verily, the brain has its "thought muscles" just as the leg has its "walk muscles." He also developed a concept of *hedonism* which stated that pleasure is the goal of life and that all motivation is selfish. La Mettrie's thoroughgoing materialism was spurned by many contemporaries as "dirt philosophy," and his influence was felt primarily among biologists.

A more interesting and influential figure during this period was Étienne Bonnot de Condillac (1754). He converted Locke's empiricism into a deterministic system of behavior hypothesizing only sensations and simple laws of association. The synthetic method of attributing sensations, one at a time, to a passive but sentient statue is the cornerstone of Condillac's psychology. Beginning with a simple odor of a rose, he proceeded to build experience into the statue by successive steps, so that the first sensation occupied all of consciousness, the second aroused a perception of a relationship and, in turn, rearoused the first sensation to produce memory, etc. Many historians ascribe an extremely important role to Condillac, because of his influence on later thought in psychology.

Charles Bonnet (1760), a Swiss naturalist and philosopher, protested Condillac's passive description of consciousness. He characterized the mind as the sum total of spontaneous reactions set off by agitations within the neural fluids. As befits such a supposition, Bonnet equipped his psychological prototype with a nervous system which functioned in much the same way that Hartley's vibrations and vibratiuncles activated the body. Bonnet is also credited with the statement, "Every sense is probably limited to different specific fibers," thus joining the anticipators of the *specific nerve energies* theory.

Even more specific than Bonnet's theorizing concerning the relationship between experience and the nervous system is the writing of French physician Pierre Cabanis (1802). Having the grisly though practical advantage of investigating the remains of decapitated humans to determine whether the victims of the French Revolution were conscious after beheading, Cabanis concluded that they were not conscious and that their random writhings were an indication that the coordinating center for the muscular reflexes must be in the brain. Upon further observation, aided by the convenience of "guillotine slips" (a macabre example of serendipity!), Cabanis suggested a physiological theory based upon the idea of levels of neural organization; in short, he attributed the endowment of graded mental capacities to the various levels of nervous-system development. His interest in the codetermined evolution of nervous tissue and behavior led, among other things, to the hope that the complexities of social interaction (including ethics) could be understood as an extension of the laws applying to individual behavior.

Other Frenchmen, like Rousseau, Buffon, Lamarck, Destutt de Tracy, and Laromiguière, might also be mentioned as contributing to the advancement of the naturalistic trend in philosophy and psychology. Some of these men are treated in greater detail later in this book.

IV. Origins of Psychology in Physiology: A Cartesian Legacy

> If I have seen farther than Descartes, it is by standing on the shoulders of giants.
>
> SIR ISAAC NEWTON

While Alexandrians Herophilus and Erasistratus (c. 300 B.C.) and Greek physician Galen (c. 200 A.D.) made significant contributions to the early history of physiology, we look to Descartes as the more conspicuous progenitor of developments in the field of psychophysiology. He undertook an analysis of the relation of nervous processes to mental processes and behavior in *Traité de l'homme* (1662). The genius of Descartes' speculations found its way either directly or indirectly into many of the topics discussed in this section.

A. Phrenology—The Localization of Higher Nervous Function

By way of preserving the continuity of thought in the general field of physiological psychology it is important to recognize the relationship between the Bell-Müller theory of specific nerve energies (to be discussed later in this chapter) and the Gall-Spurzheim conception of phrenology. Some historians have noted that phrenology, or cerebral topography, is in essence the application of the theory of specific nerve energies to the brain.

As is common with many potentially good ideas, the conception of cerebral topography evolved from a mixture of fact and fancy. The initial impetus can be traced to German physician Franz Gall's system of craniology (1810), or more popularly recognized in Johann Spurzheim's term, *phrenology*. In short, the phrenologists claimed that the hereditary development of different kinds of mental activity causes localized enlargements of the cerebral convolutions with corresponding bumps and depressions on the cranium. No fewer than thirty-seven artificial divisions of mental activity (reified "powers," or faculties of the mind) were assigned to a matching number of discrete rectangular areas of the head. Here, then, was the first elaborate system for assaying the intellectual and emotional characteristics of human beings. The early success of this theory was undoubtedly due to several factors, including Gall's status as an excellent neuroanatomist, the apparent plausibility of Gall's basic hypotheses about brain structure, the relationship between phrenology and faculty psychology, and the ease with which the theory could be substantiated (or *refuted*). Recognition of the more obvious faults of phrenology waited on pronouncements concerning the probability of statistical exceptions. A single case had been considered adequate to establish a law universal to the species. (Here we have a man who happens to possess a peculiar skull with prominent protrusions on the top of the head, and this man also happens to be devout; ergo, the bump of "Reverence.")

Popularization of phrenology through public lectures and character demonstrations by others in France, Britain, and America proved ruinous to Gall in his serious attempt to convince the scientific community. Although phrenology was *eventually* discredited by the majority of reputable scientists (e.g., the bump of inhabitiveness was formed entirely of bone, people with high foreheads were found in institutions for the mentally retarded, etc.), it provided the invaluable service of stimulating research on the problem of cerebral localization.[1]

[1] This point can hardly be overemphasized. There was serious opposition to research of this kind; for example, Scottish philosopher Sir William Hamilton, one of Gall's severest critics, argued that no assistance is afforded to mental philosophy by examination of the nervous system.

B. Advances in Brain Localization—
Physiology of the Brain

A cogent attack upon Gall's speculative notions was offered by the French investigator Flourens, who depicted the cerebrum as an essentially homogeneous organ. Luigi Rolando (1809) preceded Flourens in demonstrating, by means of crude electrical stimulation (Voltaic pile) of the exposed brains of monkeys, that the brain, as evidenced by bodily movements, responded to his efforts, the activity increasing as he approached the cerebellum with his stimulation.

Pierre Flourens's research (1824), by comparison, was neat, systematic and thorough. By means of numerous experiments, employing the novel method of *ablation*, or destruction of tissue, he found that several parts of the brain —six in all: the cerebral hemispheres, the cerebellum, the corpora quadrigemina, the medulla oblongata, the spinal cord, and the nerves—mediate different kinds of bodily activity. In working with dogs, chickens, rabbits, and pigeons, Flourens discovered a number of significant facts about the nervous systems of these animals: (a) removal of the cerebral lobes causes passivity, i.e., abolishes voluntary action; (b) injury to the central part of the medulla oblongata causes asphyxiation; (c) removal of the cerebellum disturbs muscular coordination and equilibrium; (d) removal of the corpora quadrigemina causes blindness; (e) destruction of the semicircular canals results in loss of balance. Over and above the specificity of cerebral activity inherent in what Flourens labeled *action propre* was his emphasis on the apparent integrity of the brain, an *action commune* transcending the divisible functions of its constituent parts.

In Flourens's own words we have the fundamentals of Lashley's conception of mass action and the Gestalt emphasis on field theory as it applies to the nervous system anticipated by nearly a century: "Excitation of one point in the nervous system involves all others; one point enervated enervates them all; there is community of reaction, of alteration, of energy. Unity is the great principle which rules; it is universal, it dominates all. The nervous system forms a single unified system." (Translation from *Recherches expérimentales sur les propriétés et les fonctions du système nerveux dans les animaux vertébrés*, 1824—Flourens's major report of his experimental studies.)

It is not surprising to find the close connection existing between the development of phrenology and the discovery of the so-called "speech center." In 1833, Scotsman A. Hood described one of the first accurately observed cases of aphasia (inability to use language) in *Phrenological Transactions*. The French physician Jean Bouillaud before him (1825) asserted on clinical evidence that the center for articulate speech was in the anterior portion of the cerebrum. Much later (1865) he presented a paper extolling Gall and the science of phrenology, and insisting on his own priority over the French surgeon and anthropologist Paul Broca. Because of Bouillaud's questionable methods and close tie with the phrenologists, the significance of his earlier work was not fully recognized until Broca (1861) had observed that the center for speech is located in the base of the third frontal convolution of the left cerebral hemisphere. This contention was based upon a post-mortem examination of the brain of an otherwise normal patient whose sole defect seemed to be his inability to talk for at least the preceding thirty years, and whose brain exhibited a lesion in the specified region. Broca's conclusion was unequivocally in favor of a highly localized brain. As an incidental point, it was Broca who originated the modern anthropological method of determining the ratio of the size of skull to brain.

Localization of cerebral function was given further impetus by the efforts of two German naturalists, Gustav Fritsch and Eduard Hitzig (1870). In experimental research on dogs, published in a work entitled *On the Electrical Sensitivity of the Cerebral Cortex,* they found that stimulation of certain restricted regions anterior to the fissure of Rolando aroused specific movements in various parts of the body. This significant discovery led to the localization of motor areas in the cerebral cortex. As has been already noted, Rolando had used electrical stimulation in 1809 to produce body movements, but it is to the research of Fritsch and Hitzig that one should refer regarding the importance of this method. This is brought out clearly in a statement by Harvard psychologist Edwin Boring to the effect that it was accepted dogma for most nineteenth-century physiologists that the cerebral cortex was essentially inexcitable, Rolando's work notwithstanding. The negative results were explained by Fritsch and Hitzig as due to crude methods of stimulation (largely chemical and mechanical rather than electrical) and unsystematic investigation. Here again, as Boring so aptly quotes from Flourens, "It is the method which gives the results."

The research of other investigators (among them Ferrier in England, Nothnagel and Munk in Germany, Carville and Duret in France) extended the basic principle of a highly localized central nervous system. Some of them offered diagrams of the brain with compartmentalized functional areas resembling the old phrenological drawings, the difference being, of course, in terms of the kinds of behavior mediated by the neural tissue involved. David Ferrier (1876) and Hermann Munk (1880) deserve special mention, since they were successful in identifying the highly localized sensory areas of the brain. The following list serves to illustrate the nature of these discoveries: taste localized in the gyrus hippocampi, hearing in the cortex of the temporal lobe, and vision in the cortex of the occipital lobe. Certainly, results such as these represented a continuation of the idea of exact cerebral localization.

Representing an intermediate position on localization

were the brilliant though somewhat difficult writings of the English neurologist John Hughlings Jackson (1884). Arguing along Spencerian lines, he conceived of the nervous system as a composite of higher and lower levels of evolutionary development which serve to mediate more and less complex functions, respectively. Jackson, in elaborating on Cabanis' idea nearly a century later, supposed that nervous disease was essentially a "dissolution" of the nervous system whereby the higher or more recently evolved levels become more easily deranged than do the lower ones. We shall return to this basic idea in considering the importance of the limbic and reticular nervous systems later in this section.

In re-emphasizing the generalized functions of the brain, Shepherd Franz (1907), employing the ablation technique (as did Flourens before him), reached the now not too novel conclusion that the cerebrum functions in a general rather than in a specific manner. This American's research, however, was a highly sophisticated probe into a very complicated area. For example, he removed the frontal lobes of the cerebrum from cats and monkeys and found that the animals retained well-established habits but demonstrated a loss of recently acquired habits. Franz also stressed the fact that many cases of speech impairment resulting from brain injury may be rectified through re-education, demonstrating an extremely important point that other cerebral areas may *function vicariously* for the injured portion. In more general terms, it appeared that so-called "centers" are parts of larger neural circuits and that duplication of function is not unusual in the brain.

Karl Lashley (1929), the eminent American ethophysiologist, supported and strengthened the view of the generalized nature of cerebral functions. He concluded from a brilliant series of observations on the effects of experimentally produced injuries to the brains of rats that there is a "nonspecialized dynamic function of the tissue as a whole." More specifically, Lashley's main experimental research demonstrated: (a) that learning any task, irrespective of its nature and the senses involved, is a function of the entire cortex; (b) that the ability both to learn and to retain what has been learned is proportional to the *amount*, regardless of location, of cortical tissue present (*mass action*); and (c) that a given part of the cortex can substitute for the functions of other parts which have been destroyed (*equipotentiality*). When viewed phylogenetically, there is an increase in specialization of cortical function from rat to man. Despite this apparent fact, Lashley believed that within the specialized cerebral areas of higher forms, there is a similar lack of specificity as exists for the whole cortex and the maze habits in the rat. This conclusion was disputed by others. Foremost among the critics was the Canadian neurosurgeon Wilder Penfield (1950), who provided evidence not only of detailed sensory-motor localization in man, but also convincing proof of rather precise cortical localization of auditory and visual imagery, of speech skills, of integrated memory sequences, dreams, illusions, and hallucinations. These latter phenomena were the very things that Lashley had insisted were not localizable but were functions of the brain as a whole.

In sum, we have the "swing of the pendulum" in a nutshell: toward specificity of function in the cerebral topography of the phrenologists; away from cortical specificity in Flourens's concept of *action commune*; back again to an emphasis on exact brain localization in the work of Broca, Fritsch and Hitzig, and Munk; and a swing once more in the opposite direction represented by Franz's idea of vicarious functioning and Lashley's concepts of mass action and equipotentiality. More recent research in this area suggests that the problem, especially as one moves up the phylogenetic scale, is quite complex and not resolvable on an either-or basis. It appears as though regions of the cortex which have specialized functions may have a mass function as well. Perhaps there is, as Lashley suggested many years ago, a general facilitatory influence of all cortical regions.[2] In any case, an eventual compromise does not seem unlikely.

C. Other Important Developments in Physiological Psychology

1. *Sensory-motor-nerve distinction.* It is necessary to backtrack in time to pick up some of the other noteworthy developments in physiological psychology. Although Erasistratus (c. 300 B.C.) reportedly differentiated between the motor and sensory nerves, it was not until Sir Charles Bell (1811), the Scottish anatomist, that we find an experimental exposition of this basic physiological fact.[3] Bell found that when he cut the nerves leading from the dorsal side of the spinal marrow, no muscular contractions resulted, but when he touched the nerves on the ventral side of the cord, the muscles of the body twitched immediately. From these ob-

[2] Research on brain localization has been advanced immeasurably by discoveries relating to the workings of the *limbic* and *reticular* nervous systems. The limbic system, which derives its name from Broca's term *grand lobe limbique* (1878), is an interconnected group of brain structures (main bodies include the cingulate gyrus, septal area, amygdala, hippocampus, and portions of the thalamus and hypothalamus) located in the most primitive portion of the cerebral hemispheres and having to do with the functioning of emotional and motivational states. The reticular formation, consisting of ascending and descending tracks running centrally through the entire brainstem, functions primarily as an arousal system for the forebrain. C. J. Herrick (1933), J. W. Papez (1937), H. Klüver (1939), H. H. Jasper (1949), G. Moruzzi and H. W. Magoun (1949), J. Olds (1954), and E. von Holst (1959) are but a few of the important names associated with research in these fields. With such advances in knowledge, it becomes obvious that the study of any of these "levels" (including the cortex) soon appears meaningless without reference to the others. R. A. McCleary and R. Y. Moore's *Subcortical Mechanisms of Behavior* (1965) is well worth reading in this area.

[3] Gardner Murphy indicates that Galen (164 A.D.) was also aware of the sensory-motor-nerve distinction, but he thought that any given nerve possessed, in general, both sensory and motor functions, acting as a sensory tract on one occasion and a motor tract on another.

servations, Bell distinguished between what he called the "sensible" and the "insensible" nerves.[4] The French physiologist François Magendie (1822), working without knowledge of Bell's discovery, demonstrated in a more definitive manner the same basic fact—that sensory fibers group themselves in the dorsal, and motor fibers in the ventral roots of each nerve. He is credited also with the introduction of strychnine, morphine, and compounds of iodine and bromide into medical practice.

2. *Reflex action.* The history of reflex action is long and complex, and only the most cursory treatment can be given here. Descartes is probably the first person who discussed at great length the fundamental nature of reflex action. In his *Traité de l'homme* (1662) he states (in rough translation): "Little fibers from the brain, forming the core of the nerves, run to all of the sense organs of the body. They are easily moved by the objects of these senses. Thus, a fire moves a region of skin in the foot which it touches. When the sense organs are moved they pull upon the sections of the brain from which the fibers come as one might pull the end of a rope to ring a bell at the other end. By this tug, certain pores on the internal surface of the brain are opened. Through these pores the animal spirits of the brain flow back down the nerves into the muscles of the leg which moves the bodily machine and draws the foot away from the fire."

In 1736 the French physician Jean Astruc, who coined the word *reflex*, thought of the phenomenon as a type of mirror "reflection," whereby the animal spirits of sensation, aroused as a result of external stimulation, course through the body

---

[4] Bell discovered other significant sensory phenomena. Among his more important demonstrations were the following: the spasmodic jerking from side to side of a person's eyes after rotation of the body (ocular nystagmus); elicitation of taste sensations by stimulating the papillae on the tongue; arousal of smell sensations with excitation of the olfactory nerves, and in the event that this nerve is severed only pricking and sneezing sensations result from strong olfactory stimulation. In addition, he suggested that the inner ear acts something like a musical instrument, with fibers varying in length tuned to respond to different pitches.

to the spinal cord or brain, where they are immediately reflected along other nerve tubes of the body to produce movements. Later, in 1751 Robert Whytt, the Scottish medical writer and physician, distinguished beween voluntary and involuntary activity, arguing that reflex activity is involuntary and dependent solely upon the spinal cord. Whytt also showed that if the spinal cord is destroyed reflex action is completely abolished.

The chief summarizer of research on reflex action (work of Whytt, Unzer, Haller, and Prochaska) in the first half of the nineteenth century was the brilliant English physician, Marshall Hall. He distinguished four kinds of bodily movement: voluntary (dependent upon the conscious action of the cerebrum), respiratory (automatic and dependent upon vital medullary activity), involuntary (dependent upon muscular irritability under direct stimulation), and reflexive (dependent solely upon unconscious action of the spinal cord). There followed a heated controversy concerning the nature and locus of conscious and unconscious states. Representative here was the contention of the German physiologist Eduard Pflüger (1853) that consciousness is a function of the entire nervous system; even spinal reflexes, Pflüger insisted, are conscious to the extent that they are purposive. Adding to the fray, the German philosopher-psychologist Rudolf Lotze disagreed in turn with Pflüger and upheld Hall's distinction between conscious and unconscious states. Of course, semantics played a key role here, since one's definition of consciousness, depending upon its connotations, may or may not include such phenomena as spinal reflexes.

3. *Nature of nerve structure.* German histologist Joseph von Gerlach's discovery (1858) of staining tissue with carmine (a purplish-red pigment obtained from the dried bodies of the females of certain scale insects) enabled the microscopist to probe the details of the minute structure of neural cells. Fifteen years later, in 1873, Camillo Golgi developed

a much superior method of staining nerve tissue with nitrate of silver. Using his own histological techniques, the Italian physician conceived of the nervous system as a network of axon fibers and their collaterals. Little importance was given to other anatomical structures such as the dendrites and synapse until the work of the great Spanish neuroanatomist, Santiago Ramón y Cajal (1889). In studying the frog retina, Cajal was the first to clearly differentiate the various cells involved in transmitting visual stimuli from the retina to the brain. The optic nerve alone contained five types of ganglion cells, each possessing a different shape of dendritic ending. He also discovered that each nerve cell and its related fibers form an independent unit sensitive to stimulation. Among Cajal's many theoretical contributions was the suggestion that cortical dendrites grow in response to stimuli and are dwarfed if function is absent. But Cajal was not an experimentalist and such insights remained to be validated in the laboratory work of twentieth-century researchers. Golgi and Cajal shared the 1906 Nobel prize for physiology and medicine.

4. *Nature of nerve conduction.* Discovery of the electrical nature of the nervous impulse grew out of Luigi Galvani's experiments (1791) on nerve-muscle preparations. The Italian physician and physicist produced muscle twitches by inadvertently stimulating the nerve with two different metals. Galvani thought—incorrectly—that this revealed the existence of "animal electricity" conducted by the two metals; he did not realize that his rudimentary battery was responsible for the production of the electric current. Alessandro Volta (1800), the Italian physicist, later disputed the idea of animal electricity by showing something of the true nature of electric current.

In 1841, another Italian physicist, Carlo Matteucci, by means of a recently developed galvanometer, measured what was called a "current of injury" flowing along a muscle. Building upon this work, the German physiologist Emil Du

Bois-Reymond (1848), one of Johannes Müller's students, postulated a theory anticipating more modern speculations concerning the polarization of animal tissue. Although the details of his theory were incorrect, he rendered a great service to science by helping to remove the nervous impulse phenomenon from the occult realm of animal spirits to something observable and measurable. Julius Bernstein (1866) favored the fundamentals of Du Bois-Reymond's polarization theory and, aided by an electrometer, found evidence in support of the nervous impulse as a "wave of negativity." But the largest single discovery to bring the "mind to time" was Hermann von Helmholtz's measurement of the speed of the nervous impulse. In 1845, the eminent German physiologist Johannes Müller had proclaimed that "the time required for the transmission of a sensation from the periphery to the brain is infinitely small and unmeasurable." Six years later, a recalcitrant Helmholtz not only refuted this proclamation, but found the speed of the nervous impulse to be well within range of accurate measurement with the proper instruments. This discovery had extremely important implications for physiological psychology.

5. *Theory of specific nerve energies.* Another contribution to the history of physiological psychology to be mentioned here is Johannes Müller's theory of specific nerve energies (1826) alluded to earlier. Although Bell anticipated the renowned German physiologist, we look to Müller as giving the theory more formal and universal treatment. His statement that sensation consists of an awareness of the properties of the sensory nerves themselves led to the eventual abandonment of the old *image theory* (that there exists within the mind a sentient being who receives copies or emanations of external objects transmitted via the senses) which had exerted considerable influence down through the ages. Certainly, Müller's reluctance to indicate the locus of the specific nerve energies—in the sense receptors, along the nerves, or in the brain itself—was a definite incentive to the

study of brain localization (see preface to Section A, this chapter).

Of related interest is the extension of this basic concept to the individual nerves themselves. Although Helmholtz is usually given credit for formulating the theory of *specific fiber energies,* earlier work by Natanson (1844) and the eminent German physiologist Alfred Volkmann (1845) bears on the same general point. Natanson, in particular, claimed that there are as many neural organs as there are bodily functions. At least four of the five senses could be broken down into simpler receptor units: the skin sense into fibers sensitive to temperature and touch; taste into fibers for sweet, sour, and bitter substances; vision into receptors for red, yellow and blue; and separate fibers for the simple smells. But it was Helmholtz (1863) who developed this line of thought in favoring the trichromatic theory of English physician-physicist Thomas Young (three kinds of receptors in the retina sensitive to the "principal" colors of red, green, and violet) and advancing his own *resonance theory of hearing* (the ear contains a mechanism capable of receiving all the individual vibrations in pitch—a separate fiber for some 5,000 different frequencies of sound—which the hearer can discriminate). The early date (1807) of Young's color theory suggests that he is to be included as a forerunner of the specific nerve energies concept.

6. *Theory and research on hunger.* In reviewing the history of motivation theory, one is impressed by the prophetic analysis of hunger made by the great Swiss physiologist Albrecht von Haller (1765). He considered pain arising from the peristaltic motions of an empty stomach and pleasure from the sense of taste as the primary motivators inciting the feeding response. Although physiologists since then have disagreed as to the origin of the sensations (in the stomach, Haller; in a neural "hunger center," Magendie, 1836, and M. M. Schiff, 1867; or in nerve endings throughout the body, J. Roux, 1897), they all believed that the causes of in-

gestion were those of the unpleasant sensations of hunger and the satisfying pleasures of eating and satiety.

One of the greatest general developments in motivation theory was Claude Bernard's constancy principle (1878). The eminent French physiologist is recognized as the first to indicate that the vital processes of breathing, heat production and expenditure, and eating and drinking are all regulated in the body so as to maintain the constancy of the internal environment. The concept is probably better recognized in Walter Cannon's term *homeostasis* (1932), which, in the Harvard physiologist's own words, "does not imply something set and immobile, a stagnation. It means a condition—a condition which may vary, but which is relatively constant." Another famous French physiologist, André Mayer (1901), applied Bernard's basic idea in greater detail to the study of feeding and drinking in animals. By a series of careful experiments, Mayer was able to show that tissue needs of the body could be maintained precisely over long periods of time, provided that the animal had free access to the required foods. He also discovered that animals had it in their regulatory abilities to selectively readjust bodily conditions following depletion by starvation if given the opportunity of feeding from an array of foods containing the needed nutrients.

Cannon and A. L. Washburn (1912) followed Mayer in demonstrating that the conscious sensations of hunger pangs are positively correlated with an increase in gastric motility. Later, two other American researchers, E. Bulatao and A. J. Carlson (1924), showed the accelerating and inhibiting effects of low and high blood-sugar levels, respectively, on gastric contractions. Not until recently did André Mayer's son, Jean Mayer (1952), add greater sophistication to the blood-sugar theory by postulating the existence of sugar receptors (possibly in the hypothalamus) which have the effect of monitoring the level of glucose used in the body. The existence if these "glucoreceptors" would help to explain how the body maintained its own blood-sugar level through the regulation of daily food intake.

Other investigators (including A. W. Hetherington and S. W. Ranson, 1939; J. R. Brobeck, J. Tepperman and C. N. H. Long, 1943; and A. S. Paintal, 1954) found that feeding was partly controlled by various sections of the hypothalamus: experimentally produced lesions in the ventromedial nuclei caused obesity through overeating, while lesions formed in the lateral hypothalamus brought about the cessation of eating and death from starvation. Furthermore, a psychologist at the University of Pennsylvania, Philip Teitelbaum (1962), among others, showed that when motivation for food is impaired by hypothalamic lesions, the pleasures issuing from the taste of food were necessary for caloric regulation. In general, experiments of this kind support the distinction between the peripheral (sensory) and internal (organic) determinants of ingestion which Haller favored so long ago. A more thorough history of research in this area is to be found in Mark Rosenzweig's chapter, "The Mechanisms of Hunger and Thirst," published in Leo Postman's *Psychology in the Making* (1962).

V. Beginnings of Clinical Psychology: Incarnate Human Gods to the Unconscious

> *It may puzzle some that the approach to human behavior should lead through such an apparent bypath, but a frontal attack is not necessarily the most effective. Nature's secrets sometimes yield to an ambuscade.*
> HERMAN M. ADLER

A. Historical Antecedents—Early Views of Insanity

Tracing historical roots presents the problem of exactly where to stop. The Scottish anthropologist and folklorist, Sir James Frazer, in his monumental tome, *The Golden Bough* (1890), referred to the primitive custom of regarding the insane as "incarnate human gods." Seriously disturbed persons were often given over to holy men for kind or harsh treatment depending upon whether the supernatural diagnosis indicated a godly or satanic cause of the insanity. Practices of this kind insulated the mentally ill from medicine, such as it was.

The work of the celebrated Greek physician, Hippocrates (c. 420 B.C.) represents a short-lived change in the attitude toward insanity. One of his most valuable contributions was the denial of the then popular belief in the sacred origin of disease. Afflictions of the body and mind, Hippocrates argued, arise not from the wrath of some evil spirit but from wholly natural causes. Imbalances in the four bodily *humors* of blood, phlegm, and black and yellow bile cause both physical and mental illness. The fallacy of Hippocrates' sug-

47

gestion that insanity occurs from an excess of moisture stirring in the brain was offset by his surprisingly advanced thinking on the classification and treatment of mental disorders. Employing rather elaborate daily clinical records of mental patients, he placed individuals into categories of mania (wild or violent insanity), melancholia (extreme depression of spirits), and phrenitis (inflammation of the brain, with fever and delirium). To treat melancholia, for example, Hippocrates recommended tranquillity, sobriety, a vegetable diet, regular exercise, and bleeding.

Little was accomplished toward further understanding of the problem in the next several hundred years. Moreover, it could hardly be said that Hippocrates was singularly successful in dispelling the idea that insanity was due to a vengeful fate. The Greek physician Asclepiades of Bithynia (c. 100 B.C.) did distinguish between acute and chronic mental disease, and also between illusions (false perceptions), delusions (false beliefs), and hallucinations (false perceptions in absence of apparent external stimulation). Aretaeus (c. 100 A.D.) another Greek physician, should also be cited for recognizing that mania and melancholia may at times represent two pathological states of the same mental illness. Advances such as these were easily forgotten or never acknowledged—rediscovery was a necessity.

The culmination of ancient medicine in the works of still a fourth important Greek physician, Galen (c. 160 A.D.) seem, with regard to mental disease, more an integration and synthesis of earlier principles than a true advancement. It is to be noted that Galen spoke of "temperaments" and their relationship to the emotional well-being of the individual. The person with a surfeit of blood is of a sanguineous temperament (i.e., warm, ardent, disposed to be hopeful), while an overabundance of phlegm produces the phlegmatic or sluggish individual, etc.

It was the great Latin physician Caelius Aurelianus, in the fifth century A.D., who expanded on the more enlightened principles of Hippocrates and Galen. He inveighed against the then common practice of starving, incarcerating, punishing, and generally mistreating the insane. In place of these cruel practices, Aurelianus favored the use of diet, exercise, massage, baths, fresh air, heat treatments, and, of a more psychological nature, simple psychotherapy in the form of discussion, reading, and travel. His practical recommendations, because of their highly unpopular nature, were largely unacceptable at the time. Ironical as it may seem, Aurelianus was partly a demonologist, believing, for example, that demons in the guise of men are responsible for the seduction of women.

The general attitude toward mental disease—and disease as a whole for that matter—in the Dark Ages (c. 475–1500 A.D.) was one of unenlightened mysticism; concerns of the body were relegated in favor of the spirit and soul. As in any age, there were a few dissenters. Some of the more noteworthy were the Persian physician Rhazes (c. 900), who provided regular hospital quarters for the mentally ill in Bagdad; the Arabian physicians Avicenna (c. 1000) and Avenzoar (c. 1100), both of whom fought demonology in the treatment of the insane; and the Greek physician Actuarius (c. 1270), who stressed hygiene and music in the alleviation of mental anguish. Despite these exceptions, belief in witches, vampires, devils, and the like was commonplace in theories of mental disease. Religious dignitaries of the Inquisition dealt out severe punishment to the condemned, and the details of their varied activities (the behavior, symptoms, method of conviction, and punishment of witches) were lavishly recorded by two Dominican friars (Jacob Sprenger and Heinrich Kraemer) in a book entitled *The Witch Hammer* (1489). On the side of mankind, Cornelius Agrippa (1520) and Johann Weyer (1563) revolted against the inhuman practices so graphically portrayed in this "best seller." Agrippa was a German philosopher and physician, one of the first men of persuasion brave enough to question the judgment of the religious inquisitors on matters of apparent medical concern. His Belgian student Johann Weyer championed the cause of including the treatment of behavior disorders in the practice of medicine. He maintained that so-called "witches" were actually mentally or physically ill, and their mistreatment was a grievous injustice against the innocent. Courageous as these pronouncements were, the established clerical order proved too strong a countervailing force for their acceptance.

B. Advent of Psychiatry—Classification of Mental Disorders

Virtually no improvements were made in the everyday treatment of the insane prior to the late eighteenth century. The Hippocratic theme and variations therefrom had the barest ameliorative effect on the actual care of the insane. They were still subjected to the most brutal forms of beating, purging, and bleeding. The medical profession, by and large, refused to interfere with such practices because of the seemingly demoniacal nature of the disorders.[1] But there was at least one French physician in the person of Philippe Pinel (1801) who stood out in humanitarian contrast to the prevailing attitude of his colleagues. He is often credited with being the first to establish the investigation of insanity on a convincing scientific basis. Of greater importance, perhaps, is Pinel's *lasting* influence on man's thinking in this area.

Briefly, Pinel regarded insanity as arising from natural causes (both organic and functional) rather than a manifestation of spiritual turpitude. Ministrations to the insane were to be as humane as that given to the physically afflicted,

[1] One haven of sorts was available to the mentally ill in 1547, when the Monastery of St. Bethlehem (from which we have the term "Bedlam"), in London was officially made into a mental hospital. There also is some evidence of the existence of a hospital with quarters for the mentally ill in Jerusalem as early as 490 A.D. and in Bagdad in 1000, as already indicated.

since they were of a related nature. In a dramatic gesture, Pinel, when appointed director of an institution for the insane in Paris (the Bicêtre, 1793), struck off the chains with which many had been bound. In place of harsh treatment, he gave his patients proper nourishment and rest, reasoning that many personality disorders had their origin in some physical malady of the brain. But more than this, Pinel argued, as had Hippocrates centuries before, that purely mental and emotional states could produce physiological changes leading to disturbances of the brain (i.e., functional cause of mental illness). It is of great significance that the practice of demonological psychiatry all but disappeared at the height of Pinel's career—an impressive accomplishment in light of the previous failures. Practical reforms (e.g., elimination of overcrowding and unsanitary conditions), however, were not widespread and took many years to reach into the rest of France and Europe.

Pinel also was one of the fist to stimulate major concern for the classification of mental illness. He himself devised an adequate classification system encompassing the more obvious symptoms of numerous mental disorders. *Mania* (acute excitement or fury), *melancholia* (depression and limited delusions), *dementia* (lack of cohesion in ideas) and *idiotism* (including organic dementia) were Pinel's four fundamental clinical types ascertained from careful observation of his patients. Jean Esquirol (1824), Pinel's best-known French successor, helped immeasurably in the refinement of the system and recommended the taking of daily medical records to better determine the patient's progress. Although Pinel urged medical schools to give their students clinical training, it was his protégé, Esquirol, who actually gave the first course (1817) in the clinical study of mental disease.

Similar work was being done in Germany. Wilhelm Griesinger (1824), a German physician, stressed the somatic basis of mental disease even more vehemently than had Pinel before him. This international emphasis on the somatic determinants of mental disorders did much to impress upon the medical profession that insanity was their problem and not a matter for clerical deliberations. Griesinger's somatological position also served as an effective antidote against the speculative tradition (e.g., Heinroth's religiously oriented book of 1830, which listed forty-eight separate forms of insanity) of considering every aberrant mental symptom a different disease; for Griesinger the symptom was some superficial manifestation of an underlying neurophysiological disorder.

The work of another German organicist, Emil Kraepelin (1883), swung the pendulum in the opposite direction, toward the recognition of more than twenty types of organically *predetermined* mental diseases. Renowned as a great synthesizer and psychiatric nosologist, Kraepelin laid the foundation for orderly and coherent clinical study of the *causes, courses,* and *outcomes* of various illnesses. In attempting to diagnose and classify the illness, he concerned himself with the patient's whole life. Toward this end, his greatest contribution was in the description of three types of serious mental disorders: "primary dementia" (withdrawal from reality, exaggerated daydreaming, and incongruous emotional response); "paranoia" (exaggerated self-reference evoking delusions of grandeur or persecution); and "manic-depressive" (alternating states of violent emotional outburst and passive melancholy). It can be said that these diseases have held a central position in psychiatric thought from the time they were introduced to the present day.

It is not surprising to learn that Kraepelin studied under Wundt at Leipzig. In this early research, he recognized the value of the word-association method as a means of ascertaining the effects on the mind of various bodily states. He found that experimentally induced conditions of fatigue, hunger, and intoxication interfered with a subject's powers of concentration and produced an increase in the number of outer associations (those in which only an accidental connection exists between the stimulus and response words). The word-association research of Robert Sommer (1894) supported Kraepelin's general approach by distinguishing among various mental disorders. The manic, for example, gave an abundance of outer associations (e.g., *coat-float, dog-fog*), while the catatonic responded in a predominantly irrelevant manner (e.g., *book-wind, light-square*).

The credibility of the organic approach to mental illness favored by both Griesinger and Kraepelin was strengthened by the discovery in 1913 of the cause of *general paresis*. Paresis, or *dementia paralytica*, had been recognized before this date: in 1798 it was accurately described by Haslam, a pharmacist; in 1822 it was introduced as a separate and distinct disease to psychiatry by A. L. J. Bayle; in 1857 Esmarch and Jessen concluded from clinical case histories that it was caused by syphilis (eminent psychiatrists of the day, e.g., Charcot and Griesinger, rejected this conclusion); in 1890 Krafft-Ebing discovered that patients suffering from the disease did not respond to syphilis inoculations; and finally, in 1913 the relationship between syphilis and paresis was settled by Noguchi and Moore, who found remnants of syphilitic lesions in the brains of paretics. All this made it quite plausible that organic bases might be found for other mental diseases.

C. Methodological Probes—
Animal Magnetism to Hypnotherapy

Philippus Aureolus Paracelsus (c. 1529) stirred the imagination of many with his unorthodox concoction of neo-Platonism, experimentalism, and superstitious magic. The Swiss mystic conceived of magnetism as an all-pervasive emanation capable of influencing the human body. This, coupled with the views of Helmont on *animal magnetism* (a magnetic fluid radiating from all men which may be used

by some to affect the minds and bodies of others), led the
Austrian medical student, Franz Anton Mesmer (1779), to
experiment with the ordinary magnet as a device for con-
trolling this subtle force. He found that he was able to induce
a trancelike state in some people simply by passing the
magnet over and about them—all of this accompanied by
incantations to provide the appropriate atmosphere. Later,
going to Paris both to escape the wrath of the Viennese
medical profession and to ply his trade in the intellectual
center of the world, Mesmer quickly became the darling of
the physically and mentally ill. Although Mesmer had
learned from the demonstrations of a German Roman Catholic named Johann Joseph Gassner (1776) that the human
hand contained as much magnetic power as did metal plates,
he dramatically offered his Parisian clients the mysteries of
the *baquet*, an ornate, mirror-lined tub of magnetized iron
filings, other minerals, as well as bottles, and protruding iron
rods around which the patients sat, connected to the *baquet*
by cords tied to their bodies and passing into the tub.
Cloaked in magician's garb and aided by dim lights and
wafting music, Mesmer circled the patients, touching some
on the hypochondriac region with a long iron wand or magnetized fingers, and soothing others with a softly spoken
"*Dormez.*" All in all, the effects were most successful and
scores of persons were dramatically "cured." The cure,
Mesmer sincerely believed, involved the re-establishment
of the patient's magnetic equilibrium by means of the subtle
emanations passing from the filings through the iron rods
into the bodies of the patients.

Increasing criticism of a traditionally staid medical profession resulted in the formation of a French royal commission
charged with investigating the validity of the theory of
animal magnetism. The commission, including eminent men
such as the chemist Antoine Lavoisier and United States
Ambassador to France, Benjamin Franklin, concluded among

other things, that the cures, contrary to popular belief, were not due to the mysterious forces of magnetism but to the patient's expectation or "imagination." Mesmer, who actually had not allowed the commission free access to his sessions, was forced to leave Paris. Here we have still another case of inadvertent discovery—Mesmer had hoped to validate animal magnetism, but instead created concern for the powers of suggestion.

Undaunted by Mesmer's rebuke, others carried on the illusion. Marquis de Puységur (1785) experimented with trees ("The tree is the best *baquet* possible; every leaf radiates health.") and found that they could be magnetized and used in a mesmeric fashion for effecting cures. A "control study" by Benjamin Franklin, consisting merely of telling persons that certain trees had been magnetized, provided evidence supporting the commission's hypothesis that it was the patients' imagination being stimulated and not some mysterious magnetic force. In London, an eminent English physician named John Elliotson (1837) fought a highly critical profession in attempting to establish the validity of mesmerism; and toward this end he founded the journal *Zoist* (1843), devoted to "cerebral physiology and mesmerism, and their applications to human welfare." Also in 1843, there appeared another journal, the *Phreno-Magnet*, edited by Spencer T. Hall, which represented the more popular side of the movement. In this way, mesmerism was allied with a brand of phrenology. This proved too much for the medical profession and acceptance of mesmerism was set back still further.

The change in emphasis from therapeutic tool (*à la* Mesmer and Elliotson) to anesthetic agent shed a different light on mesmerism. Discovery of its anesthetic properties is usually credited to British surgeon James Esdaile who, having read of Elliotson's work, performed hundreds of successful, pain-free operations on Indians using mesmeric analgesia in 1845.[2] Fortunately, the government reacted to a favorable committee report of Esdaile's findings by establishing a small mesmeric hospital in Calcutta. Esdaile's success was spurned by the Indian medical society, which accused him of being duped by his patients' ingratiating demeanor. Contributing to his censure in medical circles were statements such as "I am convinced that Mesmerism as practiced by me is a physical power exerted by one animal on another . . . and I should as soon adopt the diabolical theory as a satisfactory solution of the problem, as attempt to account for what I have seen and done by the action of the imagination alone" (Esdaile, *Introduction of Mesmerism into India*, 1856). His reports were barred from Indian and British medical journals, and as a result, Esdaile was prompted to publish a book describing his pioneering work in India.

Had not the use of chemical anesthetics—such as nitrous oxide (American dentist Horace Wells, 1844), sulphuric ether (American dentist W. T. G. Morton, 1846), and chloroform (Scottish physician Sir J. Y. Simpson, 1847)— been introduced when they were, the mesmeric trance as a form of analgesia might have won more favor among the medical community. By comparison, the chemical agents had none of the occult properties of mesmerism, and consequently pre-empted the field.

Where others failed, the British surgeon James Braid (1846) succeeded in gradually winning over a skeptical medical profession on the merits of mesmerism. Braid, himself a skeptic at first, steadfastly refused to believe the quasi-mystical theories of the mesmerists. After much thought and investigation of his own, he came to accept the validity of trance states but rejected the supposition that the

[2] The unprecedented discovery is hard to come by. In 1842, English surgeon W. S. Ward reported to a highly skeptical Royal Medical and Chirurgical Society that he had successfully amputated, seemingly without pain, the leg of a patient who was under mesmeric trance. The society refused to believe Ward and censured him for what some considered to be immoral medical practices (i.e., precluding pain where pain was "a wise provision of nature.")

mesmerist held some strange magnetic influence over his subject. Instead, Braid offered to the medical world a much more palatable physiological explanation of the phenomenon. His conclusion, that the mesmeric trance was essentially a sleep "caused by paralyzing the levator muscles of the eyelids through their continued action through the protracted fixed stare," was couched in terms that most medical men could accept. Elaborating on this simple notion, Braid concluded that "the whole process depended on the physical and psychical condition of the patient . . . and not at all on the volition, or passes of the operator, throwing out a magnetic fluid, or exciting into activity some mystical universal fluid or medium." As Boring comments, "modesty begets sympathy." Had Elliotson been less immodest in his protestations, he may not have incurred the wrath of his profession.

To further accentuate the break with his predecessors, Braid coined the term "neuro-hypnotism" (in a book entitled *Neurypnology*, 1856), which later was simplified to *hypnotism*. The choice of words was fortunate. Braid was a hypnotist; his predecessors were mesmerists. Guilt by association was partly avoided by a change of labels. Finally, Braid discarded his physiological theories of hypnosis, in favor of a psychological interpretation which explained all hypnotic phenomena as due to mental concentration, or *monoideism*. The fact that not all hypnotized subjects fell asleep proved the inadequacy of Braid's earlier physiological theory of nervous sleep.

In close succession came the work of French physician Ambroise-Auguste Liébeault (1866) and his colleague Hippolyte Bernheim. These men did not have to convince a hostile profession of the validity of hypnosis, but rather they had to demonstrate to the skeptics its true nature and how it could be used in therapy most efficaciously. Their main contribution was the hypothesis that both hypnosis and hysteria (functional disorders in which no apparent organic impairment can be found) are due to suggestion. Dramatic proof of this supposition came in the form of hypnotically induced and eliminated hysterical symptoms such as localized paralysis. The "Old Nancy School," as the views of these men are sometimes labeled, marked the start of a major breakthrough in clinical psychiatry. Of no mean importance was Bernheim's view of hypnosis as a form of behavior similar to normal waking behavior, capable of being produced in nearly everyone.[3]

The old became the new primarily through the efforts of French pharmacist and psychiatrist Émile Coué (1912). Hypnosis as *autosuggestion* was the cornerstone of the "New Nancy School" (also known as Couéism). While Liébeault and Bernheim had considered rapport between hypnotist and patient to be all-important, Coué asserted that all suggestion is imposed by the patient upon himself.

But all was not right. Jean Martin Charcot (1893), the eminent French neurologist, disputed the findings of Liébeault *et al.* in contending that hypnosis is a morbid state allied with hysteria, which in turn is a neurosis due to organic weakness. In a sense, then, hypnosis for Charcot and the Salpêtrière School (of which Charcot was the leader) was a physiological phenomenon to be understood as one manifestation of hysteria. Unlike Bernheim, Charcot believed that true hypnosis could be produced only in neuropathological cases. Both schools supported their views with intelligence and sincerity. This proved of great value toward the acceptance of hypnosis as a genuine medical procedure. Charcot was eventually won over to the psychological interpretation of hysteria and did much to promote the idea.

---

[3] In this sense, the views of Bernheim and Clark L. Hull (*Hypnosis and Suggestibility: An Experimental Approach*, 1933) have much in common. Hull offered experimental documentation that the phenomena of hypnosis were not discontinuous from the main body of psychological data. Treating hypnosis as the effect of *prestige* suggestion, Hull anticipated later investigators who dealt with it as an interpersonal or sociopsychological phenomenon.

D. *Culmination of a Theory—Freud*

In Freud, we encounter an institution. The adjective Freudian is as common as Aristotelian or Darwinian. Had Freud not lived, would the times have produced a substitute? Is eponym, in this case, really placebo? No answer, of course, is possible for, as historian Boring readily admits, "the dynamics of history lack control experiments." [4]

Sigmund Freud's contributions to the understanding of human behavior are truly of lasting significance. There is space only for the highlights. Much of the early history given here is taken directly from Freud's Clark University lectures reprinted in *The American Journal of Psychology*, April 1910.

In more than fifty years of active work, the famous Austrian moved from the influence of German physicalist Ernst Brücke (who, along with Carl Ludwig, Du Bois-Reymond, and Helmholtz, pledged to fight vitalism in favor of the mechanistic belief that "no other forces than common physical-chemical ones are active within the organism") to become the great expositor of psychoanalytic theory. Under Brücke, Freud engaged in orthodox medical research concerned primarily with the embryology of the nervous system. His introduction to the study of hysteria came a few years later, in the late 1870s, through his association with an older Austrian physician, Joseph Breuer. The two men collaborated in the cure of one of Breuer's patients, a girl of

[4] Boring's thesis in "Eponym as Placebo," an address before the Seventeenth International Congress of Psychology (Washington D. C., August 1963), is that eponymy distorts history. In Boring's own words, "It magnifies those persons who are found above the threshold and diminishes those below it. Eponymic distortion arises out of man's limited range or perception . . . out of his need for leaders . . . and out of his desire to perceive high goals upon which he may train his ambition." In contradistinction to this general point is a short, though incisive quote from Aldous Huxley, "The *Zeitgeist* is just Professor Pavlov."

twenty-one, who suffered from a complex of physical and mental disturbances, including such things as paralysis of both right extremities, impairment of vision, abnormal eye movements and, of particular interest, a repugnance to the act of drinking from a glass of water. It was in the tracing of this latter symptom that Breuer and Freud established what might be considered a prototypic example of unconscious motivation. In brief, the girl could not force herself to drink from a glass of water in spite of tormenting thirst. She would take the glass of water in her hand, but as soon as it touched her lips, she would push it away in utter disgust. After six weeks of this (eating succulent fruits to quench her thirst), she revealed under hypnosis an incident regarding her English governess who had allowed her dog, that the patient abhorred, to drink from a glass of water. Out of politeness, the patient had remained silent. But once the memory was revealed under the protection of hypnosis, the girl expressed in no uncertain terms her anger, and with this, the symptom vanished permanently. Breuer and Freud concluded that the symptom was a remnant, or "memory symbol," of a traumatic experience. This is thought to have been the first purposeful use of *catharsis* in the curing of hysterical symptoms.[5]

In 1885 Freud went to Paris to study with Charcot. The eminent French psychiatrist, with his demonstrations of hypnotically produced paralysis and—of greater significance to Freud's imaginative mind—the suggestion that hysteria had a sexual basis, made a lasting impression on the younger man. Returning to Vienna in 1886, Freud resumed collaboration with Breuer and, as a consequence, the two men published their most important work on hysteria (*Studies of Hysteria*, 1895). Hypnosis was their main procedure during this period of research. Freud had visited Bernheim in

[5] Freud indicates that it was the patient herself who called this new kind of treatment the "talking cure," or more facetiously, "chimney sweeping." It will be remembered that Aristotle first used the term *catharsis* (which in Greek means "purification") to apply to the effects of tragic drama.

France and had come back much impressed with the advancements made by the Nancy School. But continued use of the hypnotic method led to difficulties, the most serious of which was the fact that not all persons could be hypnotized. Furthermore, cures under hypnosis seemed to be short-lived; an amnesia might be removed, but soon after a paralysis or some other hysterical disorder would take its place.

In searching for a new method, the two men—partly because of what Freud had learned at Bernheim's clinic—allowed their patients, who were placed in a normal relaxed state, to reminisce about anything that occurred to them, permitting their thoughts to carry back gradually to the origins of the disorder. Thus, *free association* became one of the methodological cornerstones of the psychoanalytic approach. Unlike hypnosis, which served to mollify the patient's inhibitions, the new method enabled the researchers to study at first hand the key mental process of *resistance* (psychic opposition to the expression of disagreeable memories).

Freud and Breuer finally parted ways, partly because of the former's growing disillusionment with hypnosis, and more importantly because of the latter's reluctance to become embroiled in the ever-deepening emotional involvement of his neurotic patients (*transference*). What proved an encumbrance to Breuer caught the scientific fancy of Freud. The presence of resistance was undeniable proof, thought Freud, of the existence of *defense* or, as it was later called, *repression* (the process by which unacceptable desires or impulses are forced into the unconscious). The repressed desire or wish is usually represented in consciousness as a "disguised and unrecognizable surrogate-creation [Ersatzbildung]." There is no question of the central importance given this concept; in Freud's own words, "the doctrine of repression is the foundation stone on which the whole structure of psychoanalysis rests."

Freud extended his novel method to the interpretation of dreams and various acts of bungling (e.g., slips of the eye, pen and tongue, forgetting of simple things, losing or breaking objects, etc.). For Freud, nothing of the psyche is arbitrary or lawless; all acts, regardless of their superficial appearance, are manifestations of a widespread motivation. The bungling of acts, when traced to their unconscious sources, are operational proofs of the existence of repression and surrogate-creations. Dream analysis, in particular, became the *via regia* to the understanding of the unconscious. The *latent*, or unconscious, content is deciphered from the *manifest*, or disguised, symbolism. The dreams of young children are direct and wish-fulfilling, while the manifest content of adult dreams is often a conspicuously distorted surrogate for unconscious thoughts. An extremely important consequence of this new trend in methodology was the significance given to the early childhood years in the formation of adult personality.

Charcot, it will be remembered, had indicated to Freud the sexual basis of some nervous disorders. This casual observation, coupled with similar remarks by Breuer and the gynecologist Rudolf Chrobak, led Freud to one of his most important psychoanalytic beliefs: the importance of sex, particularly *infantile sexuality*, in the make-up of the psyche. The sexuality (construed by Freud in its broadest sense including erotic pleasure, love objects, homosexuality, etc.) of early childhood years sets the stage, so to speak, for later personality development.[6] At first, the infant receives satis-

---

[6] Freud credits Sanford Bell for having anticipated his position on the importance of infantile sexuality. In 1902, three years before the publication of Freud's views on the subject, Bell wrote, in a thesis entitled *A Preliminary Study of the Emotion of Love between the Sexes,* that "the emotion of sex love . . . does not make its appearance for the first time at the period of adolescence as has been thought. . . . The unprejudiced mind, in observing these manifestations in hundreds of couples of children, cannot escape referring them to sex origin. The most exacting mind is satisfied when, to these observations are added the confessions of those who have as children experienced the emotion to a marked degree of intensity, and whose memories of childhood are relatively distinct."

faction through stimulation of his own erogenous zones—genitals, rectum, opening of the urinary canal, and other sensory surfaces. From this early *autoerotism* (a term coined by the English psychologist, Havelock Ellis), the child moves to another stage, in which the parent, usually the mother, is recognized as the souce of erotic pleasure. Freud believed that ramifications of such childhood sexual attachments to the parents present the "nuclear complex of every neurosis." Normal personality development, according to this thesis, presupposes a continued education for the overcoming of childhood fixations. The *Oedipus complex* (sexual attachment to the parent of the opposite sex accompanied by hostility to the other parent), for example, must be resolved in order that the *libido* (sexual energy or driving force behind all human action) may become attached to other love objects.

Freud made great use of analogy and metaphor. The *endopsychic censor* serves to guard against the revelation of certain unconscious thoughts; the *catalytic ferment*, a term used by one of Freud's disciples, Hungarian psychiatrist Sándor Ferenczi, refers to the person of the psychoanalyst who temporarily attracts to himself the affect which is liberated in the course of therapy. The *id* (psychic reservoir of libidinal energy), *ego* (developing from the id in response to, and acceptance of, an external reality) and *superego* (the conscience of the unconscious) were also considered somewhat as one might view the operations of a boiler, or the machinations of three siametic homunculi. But, as even Freud's severest critics must concede, argument by analogy and metaphor is often helpful in the early stages of psychological theory construction. On the way to maturity, however, moltings must necessarily take place, as misleading and ambiguous terms are discarded.

The Swiss Carl Jung (1909), was particularly interested in Freud's views on dream analysis and combined them with the association method in probing the unconscious. Dreams

and myths, he believed, flow from the *collective unconscious,*
an experiential repository of human evolution which transcends the individual dreamer, society and historical epochs.
Jung's use of the association test was quite straightforward:
the patient was given a wide selection of stimulus words
and told to "answer as quickly as possible the first word
that occurs to your mind." Abnormally long delays in re-
sponding to given words were clues to hidden conflicts.
Although this was but one of Jung's many experimental
findings, he is recognized more for his rather complex theoretical contributions to psychoanalysis. Best known of these
is his dichotomy of personalities into *introversion* (directing
one's interest upon oneself rather than upon external objects
or events) and *extroversion* (directing one's interest to
phenomena outside oneself rather than to one's own experiences and feelings). The eventual break between Jung and
Freud (1911) resulted from several factors, the most significant of which was Jung's broadening of the libido concept
to incorporate all of life processes, not only its sexual component. Other, more personal matters, such as bad feelings
over the presidency of one of the international congresses,
hastened the split between the two men.

The Austrian psychiatrist Alfred Adler (1907) also disagreed with Freud on the relative importance of the sexual
libido in personality development. In Adler's *individual
psychology,* the need for superiority and power replaced
sexuality as the core impulse in the unconscious. Failure
and disappointment produce an *inferiority complex,* which
is overcome through *compensations,* such as the development of physical and mental prowess. Insistence upon the
fundamental nature of the self-assertive impulse in human
behavior brought Adler in direct conflict with orthodox
Freudian views. Considered "not in sympathy with psychoanalysis," he withdrew along with nine of his associates,
from the Vienna Psychoanalytic Society, which Freud had
founded in 1903.

Freud retained a core of faithful disciples. In 1920, he organized an inner circle (complete with membership rings) of loyal analysts: himself, Otto Rank (who withdrew in 1925, shortly after publishing his controversial views on *birth trauma*) and Hans Sachs in Vienna, Karl Abraham and Max Eitingen in Berlin, Sándor Ferenczi in Budapest, and Ernest Jones in London. Other important ramifications of psychoanalytic theory are discussed later in this book.

VI. Nineteenth-Century Developments: The Philosophy, Methodology, and Content of Early Experimental Psychology

> *La science n'est pas, elle devient.*
> PIERRE J. M. FLOURENS

A. *The Personal Equation in Astronomy—Advent of the Reaction-Time Experiment*

For the astronomer the term *personal equation,* or personal difference, denotes systematic errors in observation originating in the observer, as distinguished from those arising from instrumental and/or atmospheric conditions. Prior to 1850, the accepted technique of fixing the exact instant at which a given heavenly body crossed the meridian was the "eye-and-ear" method—a method which required the unaided observer to coordinate vision and audition in a particularly difficult manner.

Friedrich Bessel (1823), the famous Königsberg astronomer, was one of the first to take serious notice of an incident involving the dismissal, in 1796, of an astronomy assistant (Kinnebrook) because his estimate of star transits averaged eight tenths of a second later than that of the observatory director (Maskelyne). For years Bessel gathered evidence of such personal differences and using these empirical data calculated the range of variability which could be expected.[1]

[1] Errors of observation by the observer were recognized by German mathematician Johann Karl Gauss as early as 1809. He devised a mathematical formula expressing the normal range of error with which to correct his calculations. Bessel knew of Gauss's work and applied the formula for individual error.

Bessel was also interested in the etiology of the personal equation and attempted to test the validity of various hypotheses. This research led him to favor a psychological theory which ascribed a causative role to such individual differences among astronomers as were involved in the assimilation of information from the separate sense modalities. Reasoning from such a theory as this, D. F. Arago (1842) deduced that the personal equation could be substantially reduced by requiring the individual observer to attend to a single stimulus. When one observer was instructed to make a sharp noise at the instant the star crossed the meridian and another observer to record the fraction of a second at which the sound occurred, the personal equation all but disappeared.

The *complication experiment* grew out of concern for such problems. Although Herbart (1816) wrote about complication as a mental complex including processes from more than one sense modality, it was Wundt who actually studied the phenomenon experimentally. Using a device of his own design ("Wundt's complication clock," 1861), he instructed the observer to indicate the exact point on a scale reached by a swinging pendulum upon the occurrence of a click. Experiments of this sort served to emphasize the importance of attentional or attitudinal predispositions: if the observer is listening for the click, the sound becomes conscious more quickly than does the sight of the pointer, and vice versa. In short, attentional predisposition favors earlier perception via the sense modality selected.

With the development of mechanical instruments such as the chronograph it was possible to measure the *absolute* personal equation—how much the observer differs from the "true" time—rather than differences between individual observers, or the *relative* personal equation. Experiments conducted by astronomers (Prazmowski, 1854; Mitchel, 1856; Hartmann, 1858) were designed to determine the absolute personal equations for the eye, ear, and tactual senses. The size of the absolute personal equation was found to vary as a function of certain characteristics of the objects measured, e.g., size, motion, position, etc. The establishment of many such special conditions made it apparent that a psychological rather than, or at least in addition to, an astronomical analysis was required.

Helmholtz's research (1850) with human subjects in determining the speed of conduction in sensory nerves marks the earliest *reaction-time* experiments as such. Because Helmholtz was interested primarily in establishing reliable measures of nerve conduction, he considered inter- and intra-individual variability as impediments to precise experimentation. It was not until the work of the Dutch psychologist Frans Donders (1865) that definite progress was made in this field. What Helmholtz viewed as a nuisance in the pursuit of an exact and unequivocal science, Donders considered of paramount importance to the enrichment of psychology.

Three basic methods were employed by Donders: a *simple-reaction* method requiring the subject to respond (e.g., to press a lever) as quickly as possible upon receipt of a specific stimulus; a *discrimination-reaction* method in which the subject was given two stimuli and instructed to react if one stimulus was presented and not to react if the other was given; a *choice-reaction* method requiring the subject to react, say, with the right hand to one stimulus and with the left hand to the other stimulus. Donders reasoned that the exact time for the various higher mental processes (discrimination and choice reactions) could be measured by subtracting, for example, the simple-reaction time from the discrimination-reaction time for any given subject. Although the *subtraction procedure* was rejected by many researchers, it did stimulate considerable interest in such problems. Historian Gardner Murphy considers Donders' work valuable for two reasons: first, it stressed the relative importance of central nervous processes over more peripheral phenomena (such as the speed of nerve conduction) in accounting for the variability of results; second, it was a major impetus to the analytic study of time relations in higher mental processes.

B. *British Associationism—Crystallization of Empiricist Principles*

We have encountered associationism before—in the psychology of the Greek systematists and the British empiricists, to name two of its better-known proponent groups. With the advent of Scottish philosopher James Mill's *Analysis of the Phenomena of the Human Mind* (1829) we see the culmination of associationism in its more rigid and stereotyped form. According to Mill's predecessors, associationism meant two things: that every mental state is resolvable into simple, discrete components; and that the whole of mental life is explicable in the combination and recombination of these elemental states in conformity with certain laws of association. Mill simplified even this rather modest estimation of man's ideational make-up. According to his most parsimonious system, individual ideas combine as they are received, much like beads on a string, into successive or synchronous pattern after pattern. Highly abstract ideas, then, are but patterned conglomerations of simple ideas to which man has affixed various labels or names. The mind thus conceived becomes a mosaic of crystallized sensations strengthened by the *vividness* and *frequency* of the associations. Befitting such simplicity, Mill portrayed the process of association as one of *mechanical* passivity, to be understood as *mental compounding* pure and simple.

An incidental point is the close relationship between the philosophical position of Mill and that of English philosopher Jeremy Bentham. Borrowing Bentham's hedonistic principle that human actions are motivated solely through self interest, Mill developed a utilitarian philosophy in which man was viewed as a free agent capable of bringing about his own welfare if allowed self-control without governmental interference.

John Stuart Mill (1843) was also active in the utilitarian movement, agreeing for the most part with his father and Bentham, although finding fault with the pleasure-pain principle. Over and above this, he was critical of his father's static associationism, offering instead a dynamic conception of mental life. Whereas Mill senior conceived of the mind as a compound of passively acquired ideas, Mill junior depicted the mind as a dynamic process capable of working on its raw material of experiences and producing something new due to its own activity. *Mental chemistry* rather than mental mechanics was the analogy by which sensory elements become fused into percepts and concepts. The whole is more than the sum of its constituent parts. The chemistry of water, for example, in being more than or different from the mere addition of the elements hydrogen and oxygen, is a parallel case in the universe of physical matter. He added associative similarity to contiguity as the two laws governing such chemical unions of the mind.

John Stuart Mill was also quite productive in the fields of logic and epistemology. He was a thoroughgoing empiricist, maintaining that all logical inference is basically induction, the process of accumulated experience. This conclusion was based upon the assumption that nature was uniform in all its varied aspects. His famous inductive steps for discovering the relationships obtaining between phenomena include methods of logic such as agreement, difference, and concomitant variations.

Historian Boring, in calling the roll of significant personages, considers Alexander Bain (1855) the nearest thing to a psychologist we have encountered thus far in our historical review. The Scot was a man of greater consequence for psychology than either of the Mills, particularly because of his much broader psychological interests. He reintroduced physiology into English empiricism and combined it in a salutary manner with the then well-developed associationism of the Mills. Unlike the previous empiricists (Locke, Berkeley, and Hume), Bain considered the human organism capable of originating impulses, instead of being merely able to receive and respond to sensory impressions. But Bain did not rest on these laurels, for when Darwin presented his theory of natural selection as a basis of evolution (1859), he re-emphasized aspects of his psychology that were consistent with Darwinian principles. Of paramount importance in this respect was Bain's novel approach to the psychological treatment of habit and learning. Employing the genetic method, he stated in the form of a well-grounded assumption that the nervous system possesses a primitive tendency to arouse spontaneous movement. On occasion some of this spontaneous or random movement brings pleasurable consequences to the individual, and the memory of such pleasure associated with the recall of the movement rearouses the particular movement, which thereupon becomes one of man's adaptive, learned behaviors. Here is definite anticipation of the principle of *trial-and-error* learning and the law of effect. A quote from the German historian Müller-Freienfels (*The Evolution of Modern Psychology,* Yale University Press, 1935) serves to underscore the general significance of Bain's contributions to psychology: "Viewed from the historical perspective, Bain must be recognized as a potent stimulator of all motor psychology [behaviorism]. Both French and American psychologists, especially William James, were influenced by Bain in this respect, but he was scarcely noticed by German psychologists." Befitting Bain's role as "first psychologist" was his founding of *Mind* (1876), the world's first psychological journal.[2]

[2] Early developments in psychology at King's College, Aberdeen (Scotland), are noteworthy. The prolonged antagonism to psychology in Britain from philosophers of the neo-Hegelian idealistic school did not have the sympathies of men like T. Reid, A. Bain, and G. F. Stout, who all taught at Aberdeen. Reid founded the first Aberdeen Philosophical Society in 1758,

C. German Rationalism and Empiricism—Philosophy and Psychology as Inseparable

In shifting from the pure speculation of Kant to the experimentalism of Fechner and Wundt, we encounter the writing of German philosopher Johann Herbart (1816), best known as the "father of scientific pedagogy." Metaphysical considerations and the study of psychology were not distinct in Herbart's view; one presumably complements the other. Nevertheless, he responded to Kant's challenge to make psychology a quantitative—albeit metaphysical—science by devising a mathematical system of *psychic mechanics,* which, in brief, accounted for differences in the intensity of ideas. Although the elaborate system of mathematical constructions proved the least fruitful aspect of Herbart's theory, the psychology made interesting sense.[3] He conceived of man's ideational world as marked by a churn of activity in which all ideas, old and new, strive to attain, remain, or retain consciousness. Any given idea becomes a viable part of consciousness to the degree that it is compatible with already existing ideas. However, reasoned Herbart, if the ideational

---

including for its consideration questions such as "What are the parts of the body so connected with the several faculties of the mind that the destruction of those parts brings on a destruction of those faculties?" and "Do children take more after the mother than the father, and, if they do, what are the causes of it?" A century later Bain was appointed the first Professor of Logic and Rhetoric at Aberdeen and in twenty-five years at the university advanced the science of psychology immeasurably. In 1896 G. F. Stout became the first Anderson Lecturer in Comparative Psychology, one of the oldest lectureships in psychology in Britain. Editor of *Mind* (1891) and author of *Analytic Psychology* (1896) and *A Manual of Psychology* (1898), Stout left his mark on much of British psychology.

[3] Here is an example of historian Boring's "other-than" principle (". . . how often the importance of a theory in scientific progress is other than what its proponents suppose or hope"). Herbart was vehement in protesting that psychology was not the mere description of the mind, but the working-out of its mathematical laws. It was to be done in a rationalistic manner and not by experimentation, since the mind was unitary and indivisible.

make-up conflicts with the prevailing conscious state, then the more forceful ideas would dominate, while the incompatible ones would recede (though never disappear completely) below conscious level. Herbart's astute speculation on conscious and subconscious states was clearly the harbinger of later more advanced theories of the unconscious.

And finally, the concept of *apperceptive mass*, suggested by the great German mathematician Gottfried Leibnitz,[4] looms paramount in Herbart's psychologically oriented pedagogy. In its mathematical meaning, apperceptive mass was represented as the algebraic sum of intensities of various ideas above the *threshold of consciousness* (the point at which an idea shifts "from a state of complete inhibition to a state of real idea") at any given time. Psychologically speaking, it may be characterized as a mental *set*, or receptive attitude, which helps to determine the selection and interpretation of incoming sense impressions. This principle was applied by Herbart to the educational process in emphasizing the value of adequate preparation or experimental *background* for the assimilation of new and/or difficult subject matter. In a rather general sense, many of our contemporary learning concepts, such as *distinctiveness of cues* and *learning sets* are modernized ramifications of Herbart's principle.

Empiricist in science, teleological idealist in philosophy, theist in religion, poet and artist at heart, German philosopher Rudolf Hermann Lotze, (1852) was largely responsible for the interest in empiricism shown by Wundt and his immediate predecessors. But it is important to realize that Lotze's famous *local sign* theory was by no means unequivocally empirical, primarily because of his original premise

---

[4] Basic to Leibnitz's speculations concerning the process of apperception, is his acceptance of an unconscious-conscious continuum of mental life. Full awareness, or apperception, may be seen as the culmination of an infinite number of *petites perceptions*, such as the sound of individual drops of water forming the conscious actualization of the ocean surf.

which endowed the brain with an inherent capacity for spatial ordering.[5] Consequently, Lotze's theory, which in brief stated that perception is built up, or "learned," through the associations of actual movement in space with the movement-produced stimulation (e.g., the movement of the eye to focus an image, of the arm to touch an object) of local sensory spots, has also been called the *genetic theory*. Although founded on somewhat ambiguous assumptions, the genetic theory proved much more valuable than had other purely empirical or nativistic theories of space perception in pointing out the interrelation between the function of innate sensory mechanisms and actual experience with objects in space.

In a more general way, Lotze was also active in working toward the unification of psychological principles into a coherent system that would satisfy both the scientist and the philosopher. As it turned out, however, Lotze's concern for establishing correlations between mental and physical processes appears shallow at best alongside the equally emphatic Lotzian pronouncement that mere acceptance of a psychophysical relationship is not explanation in its true metaphysical meaning. Science, in its mechanistic sense, argued Lotze, could offer no insights into the ultimate meaning of life. True as this might be, the exact means by which such insights could be realized remained obscure.

D. *Psychophysics—Quantitative Attack on the Mind-Body Problem*

Ernst Heinrich Weber (1831), professor of anatomy and physiology at Leipzig, pioneered the early study of sensation, being one of the first to carefully measure the limits

[5] However, Lotze thought that space perception depends upon sensory cues which in and of themselves are nonspatial. Also, on the empiricist side, Lotze commented that pure nativism, if it be absence of theory, explains nothing.

and range of variability of certain types of sensitivity in the human being. Gardner Murphy, the American historian, points out that it is not surprising that work like Weber's came when it did—the European intellectual life for years had paved the way. Albrecht von Haller (1759), the great Swiss-German physiologist, left his mark along with the noteworthy French discoveries in physiology of the eighteenth century. It was exactly such antecedents as these that provided the *Zeitgeist* within which Weber worked.

Weber's most significant contribution, which ultimately led to the first truly quantitative law in psychology, stated that for each noticeable difference in sensation the stimulus must be varied by a constant fraction. Although this discovery issued primarily from investigations of the muscle sense by means of weight-lifting experiments, Weber did extend his study of difference thresholds into the area of visual brightness discrimination. He also devised experimental methods of studying man's ability to judge the spatial characteristics of touch sensations, including a means of ascertaining the *two-point limen* (the minimal distance between two points that gives an impression of two stimuli), and another to determine how well subjects could localize stimuli applied to the skin (*place sense*). Furthermore, Weber did research in the areas of vision (to determine the relation between the anatomy of the eye and the acuity of visual sensations), olfaction (deciding that the stimuli for smell must be in a gaseous state in order to be perceived), and temperature sense (deciding that it was due to the warming and cooling of the skin). It should be stated that Weber's more popular fame is probably the result of Fechner's further development of his basic discoveries.

The above prelude to Gustav Fechner (1860) should not be construed to mean that he was essentially a follower; nothing could be more misleading. Fechner's genius manifested itself in several ways. He began his academic career as a physician, but turned to physics and mathematics, at the same time exercising humanistic feelings in the form of satirical essays on the science of his day and serious philosophical works. The historian Müller-Freienfels aptly expresses Fechner's basic concern in the following quotation from *The Evolution of Modern Psychology*:

> It is an historical curiosity that Fechner's empiricism was ultimately rooted in metaphysical and mystical speculation; that in his microscopically exact experiments, there always lurked the tendency to prove the correctness of these cosmic speculations. Like Spinoza, he was convinced that the entire universe consists not merely of space and matter, but also of soul [panpsychism]. Parallelism does not merely exist between the human body and its consciousness but there are psychic correlations to all events in the physical world.

But Fechner was not to be remembered for his philosophical beliefs as much as for his attempts at quantifying psychological phenomena—another example of Boring's "other-than" principle of historical importance (see Footnote 3, this chapter).

Fechner attempted to establish the validity of his philosophical position (metaphysical monism) as to the fundamental identity of the mind and body through the manipulation of Weber's law. He revised the law to state that the magnitude of a sensation is proportional to the logarithm of its stimulus. Fechner argued that all *just-noticeable differences* in sensation are equal, thus providing a subjective means of quantifying sensation. The treatment of sensation as consisting of equal sense units resulted in widespread controversy (see Boring's *A History of Experimental Psychology*, 2d edition, pp. 289–295). The important thing, though, is that Fechner's status in psychology does not depend upon the validity of his formula ($S = K \log R$) [6] but

[6] S is the intensity of the sensation; K is a constant for each of the different sense modalities; R is the intensity of the stimulus. The formula is true only when the unit of R is the liminal value of the stimulus. In actuality, Fechner distinguished between "outer" and "inner" psychophysics: the former had to do with the relationship between the occurrences in the mind

with his development of various psychophysical methods, which became landmarks in the field of mental measurement (*viz.*, methods of average error, right and wrong cases or constant stimuli, and limits).

Important in Fechner's approach to psychophysics is the concept of unconscious psychical values, or *negative sensations*. Subliminal stimulation provides the energy for their existence, and their hypothesized existence the rationale for a theory of the unconscious mind. Like Herbart's incompatible ideas, Fechner's negative sensations constitute the substratum upon which the conscious mind functions.

Fechner also did research in aesthetics, which some historians believe to be the earliest systematic experimentation in this area. Among his more noteworthy contributions were such things as the use of public-opinion questionnaires to obtain impressionistic reactions to works of art (he actually polled, with little success, museum visitors on two Holbein Madonnas), investigations of masterpieces of pictorial art to ascertain the linear relations which artists had consciously or unconsciously used, and an attempt to discover through actual measurements of commonplace objects (cards, books, windows, doors, etc.) the variety of forms and combinations of lines judged to be beautiful.[7]

---

and the source and quantity of physical stimulation (R), while the inner psychophysics pertained to the relationship between the mind and the neural excitation (E) most immediate to it. In this sense, Fechner's law maintains that E is proportional to R, such that $S = K \log E$.

[7] Related to this general topic are the contributions of Louis Leon Thurstone (1927) who first used the logic of Fechner's psychophysics in studying attitudes and opinions. His aim was to provide a quantitative description of such qualitative phenomena involving scales having equal intervals and arbitrary zero points, like the thermometer. A learned account of recent advancements in this field is to be found in Stanley S. Steven's article "A Metric for the Social Consensus," *Science*, 151 (1966), pp. 530–541.

E. *Empiricist View of Perception—*
Unconscious Inference

The empirical tradition in perception has been brought intermittently to the reader's attention. One of the first major theorists in this area was Berkeley, who offered an experiential basis for space perception. Lotze's genetic theory was presented as different from, but not incompatible with, a straightforward empirical explanation. The spirit of empiricism was clearly a part of Hermann von Helmholtz's psychology which is lucidly seen in his concept of *unbewusster Schluss,* or *unconscious inference* (1866). By this term the brilliant German scientist wished to convey that the experience of space is not an inherent condition of the mind, but an inferred quality brought to present perception from the observer's past experience with objects in space. The presumption of "seen" space upon the basis of one's past interactions with objects in space is analogous to the inference that iron is hard, when it is perceived visually, because of memories of past tactual experiences with the metal. If unconscious inferences are developed through experience, then it is logical to assume that in the case of most novel experiences, and in the experiences of the neonate (newborn infant), the associations to be made are conscious. It is only through the frequent repetition of such experiences that they become automatic and unconscious.[8] Speculation of this sort, including the views of Herbart and Fechner, represents a milestone in the development of theories on the shift of mental processes along a conscious-unconscious continuum.

Needless to say, Helmholtz had a marked influence on the physiologists and embryonic psychologists of the day, and it

[8] A similar case can be made for habits. The older and more routine they become, the less the "habitué" is aware of their presence. As a matter of fact, conscious effort may at times interfere with the smoothness and efficiency of execution.

is not surprising to learn that Wundt (Helmholtz's assistant for four years at Heidelberg University) incorporated much of Helmholtz's empiricism in his own system, especially the doctrine of unconscious inference.

VII. Beginnings of Modern Psychology in Germany: Psychology as a Separate Science

> *The observer listens to nature; the experimenter questions and forces her to reveal herself.*
>
> GEORGES L. C. F. CUVIER

A. Phenomenological Tradition in German Psychology— Nativist View of Perception

Phenomenology as a systematic philosophy is attributed to the Austrian-born philosopher and logician Edmund Husserl (1901). But, as is customary, the concept as such attained prominence much earlier in the history of ideas. In 1764, mathematician Johann Lambert attached the label *Phänomenologie* to the theory of the appearances fundamental to all empirical knowledge. Kant (1786) used the term in a similar, although more restricted, sense. Much later, philosopher Moritz Lazarus and philologist Heymann Steinthal (1856) distinguished between phenomenology and psychology by maintaining that the former is concerned solely with a description of the phenomena of mental life, while the latter discipline seeks to establish causal explanations of these same mental phenomena. Treatment of phenomenology in a more methodological sense is to be found in the work of Johann von Goethe and Czech physiologist Johannes Purkinje as early as the first quarter of the nineteenth century. Both of these men insisted upon the importance of phenomenological description toward the understanding of perceptual processes. The Purkinje phenomenon, or the shift of relative brightness of colors in night vision from the red to the blue end of the spectrum, is an excellent example of the kind of basic fact about the perceptual world which phenomenology can provide.

For the philosopher Husserl, the aim of phenomenology was to analyze and describe with generality those experiences of ideation, judgment, and cognition which man conceives of empirically as classes of real phenomena. The Gestalt psychologists took over the spirit of Husserl's philosophy, favoring the unhampered description of immediate experience rather than the formal analytic treatment of consciousness in the manner of structuralism. Given this orientation, most anyone is capable of identifying certain universal principles of perception and thought without the rigorous training necessary to attain what the structuralist called a "trained introspectionist" status. Simple demonstrations suffice to convince one of such Gestalt principles, since all that is generally needed are a sketchy diagram and sensitivity enough on the part of the observer to register it. Phenomenology is nativistic (as is Gestalt psychology) in the sense that it probes little beyond givens to ascertain the developmental stages of perception.

B. The Formal Launching of Experimental Psychology— The Leipzig Laboratory

Wilhelm Wundt's revered position as an intellectual was well deserved, for his knowledge was truly encyclopedic. Writing in psychology, logic, ethics, and metaphysics, he amassed a fantastic 54,000 pages of systematically and intelligently written material. Wundt was a "repeater" in the sense that he restated many of his ideas in different contexts, constantly striving for completeness and synthesis. Some historians credit Wundt with having established psychology as a separate and viable science, as divorced from speculative philosophy (especially the variety which precludes experimentation) as could be expected at such an

early date in its development. Wundt was aware that scientists in other disciplines were making frequent use of
psychological principles in their own investigations, and he
felt obliged as the major spokesman for psychology to determine the reliability of these so-called principles. To prepare
himself for such an arduous task, Wundt studied the writing
of older scholars and followed the work of his contemporaries with critical interest. Great numbers of students con-
gregated in his classroom to hear the erudite scholar calmly
and undramatically deliver himself of his prodigious knowledge. For descriptive purposes only, Wundt's contributions
to psychology are divided here into the theoretical or systematic and the experimental. Of course, in actuality these
two aspects of scientific activity were as integrated in
Wundt's system as in others—one the complement of the
other.

As a theoretician, Wundt in 1874 proposed that psychology restrict its inquiry to the analysis of consciousness by
the method of *trained introspectionism*. Consciousness, for
Wundt, was to be studied in the form of *immediate* experience, as distinguished from *mediate*, or instrumented, experience. Once the elemental properties of experience had
been ascertained, the Wundtian approach was then supposed
to reverse the process in an attempt to fathom the manner
in which the very same elements become compounded into
consciousness as we know it. In brief, the twofold task was
first to disassemble experience into its constituent parts and
then, by reassembling the same puzzle, to discover its laws
of synthesis. Introspection was the sole means by which this
could be done.

The actual analysis of consciousness led to the postulation
of two fundamental elements, *sensations* and *feelings*. Wundt
treated sensations, or the objective contents of experience,
in terms of their inseparable properties, or "attributes,"
which he labeled *duration, intensity, extensity,* and *quality*.

Attributes were not to be construed as elements, but rather as differentiating characteristics of the various sensations. As to the affective elements, or subjective contents of experience, Wundt at first suggested a pair of feeling qualities, *pleasantness* and *unpleasantness*, but later (1896) favored a *tridimensional theory of feeling* by adding to pleasantness-unpleasantness two other pairs of qualities, excitement-depression, and strain-relaxation.[1] Just as sensations are paralleled by the physiological activity of the sense organs, feelings, according to Wundtian analysis, are matched physiologically by the fluctuations in breathing and pulse rate. Many painstaking experimental studies were done in an unsuccessful effort to establish the exact nature of this supposed psychophysical relationship.

For Wundt the integrating or synthesizing capacity of the mind involves the process of *apperception*. Herbart had written of apperception, as did the German mathematician and philosopher Leibnitz before him. However, Wundt used the term in a slightly different way to depict the process by which the elements of experience are selected, appropriated, and synthesized by the individual. Furthermore, the aspect of apperception whereby experiential elements are drawn into clear introspective consciousness was designated *creative synthesis*. In essence, then, the multitudinous elementary experiences in the form of sensations and feelings become compounded into meaningful wholes (*viz,* sensations into perceptions and feelings into emotions) by the process of creative synthesis. Theoretical issues of this sort provided the background for the vast amount of experimental re-

[1] The details of this theory led to considerable disagreement between Wundt and his most eminent student, English-born Edward Titchener. Titchener denied that the dimensions of strain-relaxation and excitement-depression were simple, affective mental processes, as Wundt believed, but instead maintained that they were "muscular attitudes" hardly deserving the status of feeling qualities. Other criticisms of this theory will be considered in the section on Titchener's version of structuralism (Chapter X).

search issuing from Wundt's laboratory founded at Leipzig University in 1879.[2]

One of the most important areas of experimental investigation involved transforming the astronomer's anathema of the personal equation into a rigorous analysis of mental functions using the *reaction-time* technique. Wundt extended the contributions of Helmholtz and Donders by attempting to determine, with little success, the portion of total reaction-time occupied by the several mental functions. In this endeavor he made use of the subtraction method (similar to what Donders had proposed), which was later to be severely criticized by Oswald Külpe, among others. In related kinds of studies, Wundt and his students found that in cases of simultaneous presentation of two stimuli one of the stimuli is perceived before the other in the event that it had been expected and attention had been directed to it. Experiments of the complication sort (see page 67) were conducted in an attempt to determine the exact nature of this phenomenon and help substantiate this theory of *prior entry*.

Wundtian supervised research on the sense modalities was diverse and of considerable merit. In vision, Wundt was one of the first to utilize in his experimental investigations the newly acquired fact of the photochemical action in the retina.[3] Experiments were also conducted to determine the relative influence of convergence and accomodation in the visual perception of depth. The results demonstrated that finer discrimination was possible when the eyes were allowed to converge, especially for movements toward the eyes. Studies in audition were used primarily to investigate psy-

---

[2] It should be noted at this point that as an experimentalist Wundt was primarily concerned with studying the *general* nature of the mind and not individual differences as such. This proved to be a significant deterrent to the development of differential psychology in Germany (see Chapter IX).

[3] Physiologist Franz Boll (1876) discovered the photochemical action in the retina. This fact was substantiated by histologist Wilhelm Kühne (1877), who focused bright lines on a rabbit's eye, then immediately excised the eye, placed the retina in a fixative and found corresponding lines bleached on the receptor.

chophysical problems. Results of these studies partially refuted the Weber-Fechner law in that observers asked to judge the midpoint beween two tones usually chose a tone that approximated the arithmetical rather than the geometrical mean. Suffice it to say that so much experimentation came from the Leipzig laboratory that in 1881 Wundt was encouraged to found the first German psychological journal, *Philosophische Studien,* as a medium for this proliferation.

A view of Wundt's work, even as cursory as this one, would hardly be just if it failed to mention his writing on racial psychology. Hans Volkelt, who studied the role that racial psychology played in Wundt's intellectual development, maintained that as far back as 1860 Wundt had conceived the plan of "adding a sort of superstructure" to laboratory psychology in the form of empirical data from anthropology and history (i.e., social psychology from the standpoint of cultural products). But it was not until the early twentieth century that such intentions were realized in ten volumes of *Völkerpsychologie.* This is certainly substantive proof of Wundt's belief that man's higher mental processes could be thoroughly studied only within an anthropo-historical frame of reference.

C. *Act versus Content Psychology—Brentano versus Wundt*

A rather well-developed act psychology can be traced to the unorthodox neo-scholastic scholar Franz Brentano (1874). As a Catholic priest for nine years (abandoning it because of his opposition to the doctrine of papal infallibility), he was well acquainted with the Aristotelian and Scholastic brands of psychology, which viewed consciousness not as an immanent condition but a state which, in all its aspects, focuses upon something extrinsic to itself. Elaborating on this belief, Brentano developed his own doctrine of the *intentional inexistence* of psychic phenomena. Consciousness, thus conceived, is not self-contained (as are physical phenomena) but contains its object within itself intentionally. With this as groundwork, Brentano argues that the *mental act* (e.g., the act of seeing a red color patch, or wishing for an object) rather than the *content* of the mind (e.g., the red color patch, or the object per se) is the proper subject matter of psychology. Furthermore, the study of mental acts is psychology, and investigation into the matter of consciousness, which is the object of the act having intrinsic completeness, is physics. Wundtian attempts to anatomize the mind were considered to be on wholly mistaken lines.

Brentano went beyond philosophical polemic to elaborate upon the implications of his controversial position. Acknowledging the need for the analysis of mental acts, he distinguished among three basic classes of process elements: *ideas* (sensing and imagining), *feelings* (loving, hating, etc.), and *judgments* (rejecting, recalling, etc.). Although Brentano left many gaps in his system (compared to Wundt's), he did raise some very interesting problems. For example, unlike the content psychologists, Brentano asserted that every idea includes, in addition to itself, an idea of itself. A corollary of the doctrine of the intentional character of consciousness, this conception was foreign to the Wundtians, who considered only the substantive idea, not the process of having the idea itself, as consciousness. Emphasis on the process of mental life might be considered the essence of act psychology. Feelings and judgments were treated in much the same manner as was the element of ideas, all three not to be thought of as substantive entities (as they were for the Wundtians) but rather as three distinguishable facets of a cohesive mental act.

Brentano was also in opposition to Wundt's overzealous use of introspective experimentation: he was in agreement that experiments should be used in deciding between two conflicting hypotheses (*experimentum crucis*), but not in sterile pursuit of the systematic. The Wundtians could hardly be more opposed to Brentano on this issue.[4]

D. *Ramifications of Act Psychology*

1. *Content as preperceptual.* Brentano's influence was considerable. We have space for only a few of his more eminent disciples. Carl Stumpf (1883), agreeing with Brentano, but in deference to Wundt, attempted to incorporate features of both act and content psychology in developing a more satisfactory system. Conceiving of mental content in the form of sensations and feelings was essential, argued Stumpf, but only as raw material upon which the mind acts. In other words, the substantive ingredients of the mind are *preperceptual,* and studying them alone—that is, divorced from the mental forces which mold and fashion them into intelligible consciousness—was at best propaedeutic to a comprehensive understanding of cognitive processes.

Having broadened the scope of psychology, Stumpf proceeded to outline in some detail what it was that psychologists should be doing. He accepted for careful scrutiny both mental content (or what he preferred to call "phenomena") in the Wundtian sense and Brentano-like acts (or "psychic functions") of perceiving, comprehending, judging and feeling. A major conclusion, based partly upon controlled introspective observation, was that events of the conscious mind are never experienced in isolation. There is no doubt of Stumpf's predilection for act psychology.

As for actual experimental subject matter, Stumpf was

[4] The relationship between Brentano's act psychology and Husserl's phenomenological approach is apparent even to the casual reader; this is not surprising, since Husserl was a student of both Brentano and Stumpf. Under Brentano's influence at Vienna, Husserl wrote *Philosophie der Arithmetik* (1891) which concluded that the laws of logic were basically psychological in nature. Husserl spent the rest of his professional life refuting this conclusion in defending the "purity" of logic against "psychologism."

chiefly interested in music and sound (his major work being *Tonpsychologie*, 1883 and 1890), and in this he ranks close to Helmholtz in renown. He applied his theory of the interplay between psychic content and function in disputing Helmholtz's physical theory of consonance. The physical theory accounted for consonance in terms of the objective characteristics of successive sound waves, whereas Stumpf maintained that consonance results from the mental act of fusing tones into such unity that the tones appear as a single experience to the observer.

2. *The Würzburg School.* Latvian-born Oswald Külpe also roamed on both sides of the theoretical fence. As Wundt's second assistant at Leipzig, he developed a strong interest in the brand of rigorous experimental psychology practiced in Wundt's laboratory (becoming disillusioned with the simplicity of the subtraction procedure); as an act psychologist, he attempted to submit the higher thought processes—Wundt's ban notwithstanding—to introspective attack. While at the University of Würzburg (1894–1909), Külpe and his associates (Ach, Marbe, Mayer, Orth, Watt) undertook a research program involving a direct introspective assault upon thinking, which yielded surprising, if not embarrassing, results for the content psychologists. Unlike the Wundtians, who asserted that all thought could be reduced to sensory, and consequently imaginal, elements, the psychologists at Würzburg found that some thoughts occur without any noticeable sensory or imaginal content. Their experimental technique consisted of presenting a trained introspectionist with a mental problem to which he had to seek an answer, as well as to observe the conscious process involved. Exact records were taken of his statements and later analyzed for an understanding of what occurred. Orth and Marba reported that during the actual performance of the task the consciousness of the problem persisted in nonsensory fashion (referred to as *conscious attitudes*, involving states of doubt, uneasiness, difficulty, hesitation, in-

capacity, etc.) although imagery of various kinds related to the problem was also present. Of considerable importance along these lines is the work of Narziss Ach (1905). In addition to researching into the nature of conscious attitudes he found that there are numerous mental predispositions which operate in an unconscious way to control the course of thought. To these unconscious mechanisms, Ach gave the name *determining tendencies*. Of a related nature were the contributions of Karl Marbe ("level of consciousness") and Henry Watt (*Einstellung*, or "task set"). In sum, the Würzburgians argued that consciousness cannot be understood by means of consciousness alone; an active mental process seems to be at work behind the scenes.

Considerable controversy resulted from this discovery, the most trenchant criticism coming fom Titchener, Wundt's most renowned student. From America Titchener issued a blunt denial that there was any such thing as nonsensory, or *imageless*, thought. All that the Würzburg School had demonstrated, argued Titchener, was shoddy techniques of introspection. In his view the Würzburgians had succumbed to the *stimulus error*, whereby the subject erroneously attends to the meaningful characteristics of the object he is instructed to observe rather than his own sensory processes. Titchener's students (Clark, Jacobson, Okabe, Pyle), on the other hand, did not obtain results indicative of imageless thought—this in itself is an interesting aspect of the controversy, i.e., the curious fact that the sophisticated subject usually found what the experimenter desired and proposed! (Seemingly a contemporary problem in which the biased experimenter makes "discoveries" supporting his theories.) In any case, it should be recognized that the experiments conducted at Würzburg incited considerable experimental interest in the more subtle (and less manageable) features of cognition.

3. *Precursors of Gestalt psychology*. Questioning Wundt's system from another, though related, position were two fore-

runners of Gestalt psychology, Mach and Ehrenfels. Needless to say, Gestalt-like concepts abound in the theoretical speculations of others we have considered thus far. A thorough tracing of its development would include, as a bare minimum, discussions of Plato's *Psyche,* Aristotle's *entelechy,* Saint Augustine's conception of the unified nature of consciousness, Wundt's *creative synthesis,* all of which bear a marked resemblance to the more modern Gestalt concept.

Ernst Mach (1885), an eminent Austrian physicist by profession, probably presented the first clear exposition of the Gestalt phenomenon as it applied to perception. He argued that certain arrangements of elements—for example, lines and angles in a geometrical figure—cause the emergence of different "totals" reported by the observer as squares, triangles, circles, etc. Paradoxical as it may seem, Mach's stand, in conceiving of the new or different totals as still another sensory content (in keeping with the Wundtian tradition), represented a theoretical position in psychology that was for all intents and purposes antithetical to the eventual developments in Gestalt psychology. It must be emphasized that Mach favored a psychology of sensation, the doctrine that all knowledge is sensorial.[5]

Christian von Ehrenfels (1890), a student of the Brentano school, incorporated the fundamentals of Mach's view epitomized in the term *Gestaltqualität* (form-quality). Transposability, a convenient example, was offered as characteristic of such readily perceived phenomena as a melody remaining unchanged though transposed into a different key with no single note of the original score recurring.

[5] Mach's range of interests was truly remarkable. For example, in physics he influenced and, some believe, anticipated Albert Einstein's views on relativity; in philosophy of science he was probably the inspiration for the quantum mechanics of Werner Heisenberg and the formation of the famed international group of scientists, engineers, mathematicians, and philosophers called the "Vienna Circle"; in physiology he displayed a knowledge so extensive and profound that William James, upon hearing Mach lecture, commented that "he apparently has read everything and thought about everything."

Boring, the American historian, is quite explicit in stating that even Ehrenfels failed to break completely from Wundt's elementarism in not making the concept *form-quality* the core of an independent psychological system. Were Mach and Ehrenfels, as historian Gardner Murphy suggests, engaged in the futile gesture of buttressing a tottering structuralism by the addition of superordinate elements? Regardless of the answer, a more definitive position on the nature of form and the laws by which it could be understood waited upon the pronouncements of other men.

Alexius Meinong, best known as the founder of the first Austrian psychological laboratory at Graz in 1894, actually came somewhat closer to the Gestalt position than did either Mach or Ehrenfels in recognizing the importance of the perceptual act itself as giving rise to form-quality, or as Meinong preferred to call it, "founded content." "Founding content" was Meinong's word for Ehrenfels' *Fundamente*, or the sensory raw material of founded content.

E. *Early Development of the Psychology of Learning— An Experimental Attack on Higher Mental Processes*

The psychology of learning, as a separate field of interest, made little headway in the laboratory prior to the advent of Hermann Ebbinghaus (1885). It will be recalled that Wundt's stand on this matter left little hope for an experimental attack upon man's higher mental processes. It was Ebbinghaus who, inspired by a chance reading of Fechner's mathematical approach to psychological problems (*Elemente der Psychophysik*, 1860), questioned the Wundtian decree in an effort to submit more complex cognitive functions to quantification.

Without the direct stimulation—so it is believed—of an academic setting he invented such important methodological tools as the *nonsense syllable* (a simple, practically meaningless unit composed of a vowel between two consonants), the technique of *constant-stimulus presentation* (in presenting a series of stimuli, each stimulus is exposed for an equal period of time; G. E. Müller and F. Schumann automated this device), and the *derived-list method* (discussed in more detail below). He also invented the *savings method* (the difference between original learning and relearning to the same criterion) to permit a reliable analysis of results. Aided by these research devices, Ebbinghaus conducted a long series of experiments examining variables such as the rate at which associations were formed and forgotten, where errors were most likely to occur, and the significance of repetition in learning. For this research, he served indefatigably as both experimenter and subject, a procedure which, for purposes of experimental control, necessitated long bouts of disciplined living. Results of his research may be broadly subdivided into factors affecting learning and factors affecting retention.[6]

Concerning the first category of variables, Ebbinghaus found a positively accelerated function existing between the length of lists of nonsense syllables and the number of repetitions required for an errorless repetition. Also, the average time per syllable was markedly increased by lengthening the list. Another series of studies concerned with the conditions of learning utilized derived lists to ascertain the presence of remote associations (this research represented, in some ways, an experimental test of Herbart's theory of psychic mechanics). In short, this method involved making up lists of nonsense syllables based upon already learned ones so that some of the lists would consist of every other item of the original, others of every third item, etc. If the derived lists of syllables could be learned faster than the equally long

---

[6] No attempt shall be made to summarize all of Ebbinghaus' results. Those who are interested may refer to a Dover edition of the original work (*Memory: A Contribution to Experimental Psychology*, 1964), or an excellent review, including the results of subsequent studies on the same issues by Robert S. Woodworth (*Experimental Psychology*, 1938).

original or completely new ones (and they were), then it stands to reason, thought Ebbinghaus, that some associations were formed in addition to those between adjacent items.

As to the second category of research, studies were done in an effort to determine the exact conditions affecting retention, including such investigations as discovering the relationship between the degree of initial learning and subsequent retention. Using the savings method, or method of relearning, Ebbinghaus established quantitative data demonstrating the beneficial nature of overlearning on retention. Of course, the most famous empirical fact born of this concern is Ebbinghaus' *curve of retention*, which shows an initial drop-off in the amount retained followed by a negatively accelerated loss with increasing time from original learning.

Some historians contend that Ebbinghaus shirked the scientific responsibility of teasing from his data the rational frame of reference which helps explain and give birth to new hypotheses. His great strength lay, rather, in the elaborate care with which he designed, controlled and conducted the experiments. Ebbinghaus' ingenuity as an experimenter is particularly impressive considering his was largely a pioneering effort. What better tribute to a man than to cite his own prophetic epigraph to his classic work on memory, *De subjecto vetustissimo novissimam promovemus scientiam* ("From the most ancient subject we shall produce the newest science"—translated by historian E. G. Boring).

Georg Elias Müller (1894), who is second only to Wundt in the breadth of his experimental program in psychology, added significantly to the work of Ebbinghaus. Considered to be the vanguard of sensory psychology because of his vitriolic criticism of Gestalt theory, Müller developed his theory of *complexes* in direct opposition to the Gestalt account of perception. The theory is too involved to review here, but, in essence, the main contrast between the two approaches is that Müller leaned toward empiricism (e.g., asserting that sensory and emotional elements must be united into groups by acts of attention), while the Gestalt theorists adopted a nativistic interpretation of perception. Furthermore, Müller claimed that he and his students (e.g., Erich Jaensch—*eidetic imagery;* and E. Rubin—*figure-ground*) anticipated most of the fundamental concepts of Gestalt psychology.

Concerning contributions within the field of learning, Müller (who did much of his own research) and his students offered the *Treffermethode,* or method of right associates, which involved, first, learning pairs of syllables, and then recalling one of the syllables upon presentation of the other. Both accuracy of recall and reaction time were recorded. This method, in addition to those invented by Ebbinghaus, were used by Müller's associates and others to probe the complexities of associative learning. Some of the better-known examples are: W. G. Smith's discovery (1896) that early and late syllables in a list are fixated more quickly than those in the middle of the series (relating to factors of *primacy* and *recency* as they apply to the *serial-position effect* in verbal learning); A. Jost's law (1897) that when two associations are of equal strength, a repetition strengthens the older more than the younger; A. Pilzecker's use of reaction times to indicate the strength of word associations (1900); and L. Steffens' research (1900) demonstrating the general superiority of "whole learning" over "part learning."

Müller, with the help of Lillien Martin, also elaborated upon Fechner's psychophysical methods, especially the method of constant stimuli (which had been previously called the method of right and wrong cases). While Fechner's original procedure involved comparing only two stimuli at a time, Müller's adaptation allowed for the simultaneous comparison of several stimuli with one standard stimulus, resulting in a more accurate estimation of subjective judgments.

VIII. The Biological Point of View in Psychology: Man as Part of the Animal World

> *The noblest study of mankind is Man, says Man.*
>
> JAMES THURBER

> *And what evolution has found wise in the past, wise in generality, wise in all the ancient sortings, these things must we bear —whether we be lion or trout or cow or kob—in the particularity of our fleeting hour.*
>
> ROBERT ARDREY

A. Antecedents

1. *The early cosmologists.* A rich source of speculation concerning divergence in nature is to be found in early Greek philosophy. The Ionian cosmologists in the sixth and fifth centuries B.C. were divided on the issue of basic cosmic elements. The monists (Thales, Anaximenes and Anaximander), it will be recalled, insisted upon a single basic element for all organic and inorganic existence. Pluralists like Empedocles and Anaxagoras insisted upon the reduction of all earthly matter to several basic elements. It was just such controversy over the essence of things that seemingly sparked the philosophical concern for the similarities and/or differences among animals.

Although most philosophers disassociate themselves from the rather direct approach taken by the ancient cosmologists, remnants of such discord are evident in more modern philosophical controversies on animal life. Examples of such include the dispute between the mechanists and the vitalists (do all living phenomena consist merely of material in motion operating mechanically, or is there some "vital force" that transcends the physiochemical aspects of life?), and the associationist-Gestalt disagreement over the make-up of mental life (is the mind essentially an amalgam of ideas fused as a consequence of experience, or a unity of forms in which the individual ideas are drawn together by higher integrating powers of the brain?).

2. *The Greek systematists.* Concern for the diversity of living things was a part of the sophisticated philosophical approach of Plato and Aristotle. In developing an evolutionary conception of different kinds of being, they (380 B.C.) distinguished between plant, animal, and human life. Fundamental to this differentiation was Plato's belief that the "soul" (or Form of life) consists of the rational and the irrational, the latter subdivided into passionate and appetitive parts. Man, according to this theory, possesses all three souls, each located in a different part of the body—the rational soul in the head, the passionate soul in the heart, and the appetitive soul in the abdomen. Animals, it was implied, are endowed with only the two lower souls, while plants, being most primitive, have only nutritive souls. Superficial differences among these various kinds of life lent a measure of credence to such speculative notions.

Aristotle (335 B.C.) insisted that philosophy develop an empirical foundation for its theories. Empiricism was also a prerequisite to progress in the biological sciences. Aristotle himself contributed significantly to this end by describing no less than five hundred different species of animals. This work—though fraught with faulty observations, anecdotal reports (e.g., "the male has more teeth than the female in man, sheep, goats, and swine"), and anthropomorphic reasoning—represents a major break from earlier thinking. The validity of Plato's soul theory, for example, depended upon a form of rationalism that disparaged empirical verification, while the credibility of Aristotelian theories was due partly to the groundwork of accumulated fact. Of course, facts are meaningless in and of themselves; it is the particular frame of reference that renders them meaningful.

Many of Aristotle's erroneous conclusions about life processes stemmed from his attempts—his empiricism notwithstanding—at justifying some preconceived notion about existence. This is to be seen in his discussion on the localization of certain bodily functions. The heart, for Aristotle, was the seat of all higher psychical processes, because it appeared to be the first organ to manifest life in the developing embryo. This conclusion was based on actual observations of chick embryos and the Pythagorean speculation that the geometrical center of forms is the most important location in the form. The brain, in contrast, was believed to be a cooling mechanism for the body and, since it was insensitive to touch, in no way connected to any of the senses. In support of the refrigerating function of the brain, Aristotle explained tears as the condensation of blood vapors in and around the head region.

Aristotle also advanced a theory of evolution based upon his philosophical position of causes. He proposed that plant, animal, and human life comprise one continuous series from lower to higher forms. Each form within this series strives for its own perfection (Ideal Form) and in this way becomes a discrete being. The theory is somewhat uncertain, because Aristotle appears to have underscored *intra-* rather than *inter-*species development—i.e., although higher forms derive their matter from lower forms (philosophically speaking), biological "movement" is hypothetically restricted to the development of the individual species. Aristotle's view on "fixed" species is in interesting relation to those of his predecessor, Empedocles, who also entertained an evolutionary theory of the origin of life. According to Empedocles, the formation of organisms starts abiogenetically from cosmic dust and develops through gradual stages whereby segments of intact bodies (arms with legs, heads with feet, etc.) become attached randomly until a combination of parts capable of survival in its environment is realized.[1] Both Empedocles and Aristotle contributed significantly to our modern conceptions of biological evolution.

3. *Alexandrian science.* It will be recalled that the Egyptian city of Alexandria became a cultural capital under the rule of the Ptolemies. It was not only a center of mathematical studies in the East, but also a haven for the sciences created by Aristotle.

Herophilus and Erasistratus (c. 300 B.C.) contributed significantly to both anatomy and physiology, being among the first to perform experiments *in vivo*. Among their more important contributions to the history of comparative psychology was their emphasis on the greater anatomical complexity of man's cerebral cortex as compared with that of infrahuman animals; thus implying an advancement in nervous function as one ascends the evolutionary ladder. Another important consequence of this research is the rejection of Aristotle's view concerning the location of the thinking force—the Alexandrians returned it to the brain.

4. *The Middle Ages.* The several hundred years following

---

[1] A similar view of evolution was held by the noted Roman poet Lucretius (c. 70 B.C.). An excerpt from the fifth book of *De rerum natura* (*On the Nature of Things*) spells out in literary fashion his position: "And many monsters too the earth at that time essayed to produce, things coming up with strange face and limbs, the man-woman, a thing between the two and neither the one sex nor the other, widely differing from both; some things deprived of feet, others again destitute of hands, others too proving dumb without mouth, or blind without eyes, and things bound fast by the adhesion of their limbs over all the body, so that they could not do anything nor go anywhere nor avoid the evil nor take what their needs required. Every other monster and portent of this kind she would produce, but all in vain, since nature set a ban on their increase and they could not reach the coveted flower of age nor find food nor be united in marriage. For we see that many conditions must meet together in things in order that they may beget and continue their kinds; first a supply of food, then a way by which the bird-producing seeds throughout the frame may stream from the relaxed limbs; also in order that the woman may be united with the male, the possession of organs whereby they may each interchange mutual joys." Anaximander also espoused a related conception of evolution.

the anecdotal research on the sagacity of higher animals by Roman scholar Pliny the Elder (c. 50 A.D.) and Greek biographer Plutarch (c. 100 A.D.) were devoted largely to activities of theological significance. Much of the scientific writings of the Greeks and Alexandrians, especially that running contrary to religious dogma, was under harsh censorship in Christian lands. In effect, the Church assumed dictatorship over what man should believe, and the final authority on all matters, natural and supernatural, was the clerical interpretation of the Bible. Occasional breaches in Church control are evidenced in the writings of such men as Saint Augustine (396 A.D.), Saint Albertus Magnus (1230), and Saint Thomas Aquinas (1257). Although most of their psychological discourse was devoted to questions of human consciousness and its relation to religious awareness, they did much to re-establish the Aristotelian teachings on nature and animal life. Unfortunately, however, the churchmen espoused more of Aristotle's "facts" than of his spirit of empirical inquiry. Strict adherence to dogma irrespective of its origin is hardly the handmaiden of success in the sciences.

The concoction of Aristotelian and Christian thought caricatured animals as dominated by blind instinct divinely implanted, and man as a rational being whose capacity for voluntary activity presupposed moral and spiritual responsibilities.

5. *The Renaissance.* The spirit of unbiased observation in the natural sciences returned to the forefront in the efforts of several outstanding men of the Renaissance. Konrad von Gesner, the sixteenth-century Swiss naturalist, championed empiricism in zoology; Bacon (1620) wrote convincingly on the value of the inductive method and argued that man should study the natural history of animals to better ascertain their relationship to one another and to man himself; Descartes (1630) fought for the liberation of science from Church dogma and developed a thoroughgoing view of animals as automata controlled entirely by instincts and re-

flexes. Other intellectual leaders of the Renaissance, such as Spinoza (1665), Leibnitz (1675), Hume (1739) and Kant (1775), added their literary talents in emphasizing the need for an unencumbered, scientific look at nature.

Along with this expansion of philosophical interest came a considerable amount of actual spadework. Carolus Linnaeus, the eighteenth-century Swedish botanist, offered a classificatory system in which each species receives two Latin names, that of the genus to which it belongs and that of the species itself—e.g., *Felis leo* for the lion, *Sorex araneus* for the common shrew, *Homo sapiens* for man, etc., Linnaeus, 1758. (For more on classification and the concept of species, see A. J. Cain, *Animal Species and Their Evolution,* 1954.)

The entire school of late eighteenth-century French naturalism, including such men as La Mettrie, Condillac, Bonnet (actually a Swiss), Buffon, Cabanis, and Destutt de Tracy, conceived of the bodies of man and the animals as quasi-mechanical systems of receptors and effectors connected by clusters of nervous organs whose purpose is to handle the input and output of energy.

B. *The Theory of Evolution—Biological Adaptation and the Organization of Psychological Processes*

Evolutionary theory in the sciences had been around a long time before Charles Darwin, the great English naturalist, appeared on the scene in the mid-nineteenth century. We have learned that the ancient Greeks had incorporated elements of the idea in their cosmological systems. In astronomy, Pierre Laplace (referred to as the "Newton of France") suggested a hypothesis for the evolutionary formation of the stars and planets. According to his "nebular hypothesis," the stars and planets are formed out of primal nebular matter which in rotation throws off successive rings of burning substance that later collect, cool, and form the heavenly bodies.

Scottish geologist Sir Charles Lyell, also in the early part of the nineteenth century, put forth an evolutionary theory suggesting that the earth itself had gone through an orderly series of changes taking considerably longer than the six days allowed by the Book of Genesis.

In biology proper, the efforts of many men helped to pave the way for Darwin's revolutionary views. Georges Buffon (1749), in attempting to advance evolutionary theory as well as placate the Church authorities, argued that God probably created only a single form of life and then allowed it to vary in multitudinous ways. He anticipated Darwin in considering morphological variability among species as a means of adjustment to the vagaries of nature. Goethe, the German literary giant, and Erasmus Darwin (Charles Darwin's grandfather) proposed similar views on the metamorphosis of body parts and the transmutation of species. Basic to these suggestions was the idea that biological characteristics of any species of living matter undergo modification as the result of adjustment to an ever-changing environment. Herein lies a fundamental principle of the more modern view; however, the times were not receptive to such revolutionary concepts, especially in the absence of supporting evidence.

It was not until the late-eighteenth- and early-nineteenth-century work of French naturalist Jean Baptiste Lamarck that the evolutionary view in biology began to gel. The French naturalist not only elaborated on what Goethe and Erasmus Darwin had said, but also provided corroborating evidence in the form of field research. His theory entailed three conditions: (a) an organism, in an attempt to satisfy its needs, must adapt itself to numerous environmental situations; (b) these situations, which demand adjustment, cause the animal to exercise certain parts of its body; (c) the exercise of certain body parts causes those parts to develop gradually and pass on to the progeny as *acquired characteristics.* The last condition gave rise to considerable controversy among biologists of the period. Georges Cuvier, another eminent French naturalist, criticized not only the Lamarckian hypothesis, but also the whole of evolutionary theory, as he upheld a religiously more acceptable theory of the *fixity of species*.

The hypothesis of the inheritance of acquired characteristics came under particular criticism with the development of genetic theory. German biologist August Weismann (1892), the genetic determinist, maintained that genetic structure is in no way altered by the kinds of conditions Lamarck had considered. Lamarck's hypothesis did not die here; certain aspects of it were incorporated into Russian biology (Lysenkoism) and remained until recent times, in sharp contrast to Western conceptions of evolutionary change. Antigenetic Lamarckism was also supported in American psychology by William McDougall, as we shall see later in this section.

It was probably Charles Darwin's impressive documentation rather than his theoretical speculation on evolution that deserves special admiration. For thirty years Darwin patiently collected data in support of a theory that had been around—albeit in a fragmentary state—for some time. In tracing the history of Darwin's own thinking, we might start with his chance reading of English economist Thomas Malthus' *Essay on Population* (written in 1798) shortly after returning from a five-year data-collection trip in the South Seas.[2] Malthusian doctrine, that human populations increase geometrically while food production increases arithmetically, suggested to Darwin the struggle for existence of all living things and the survival of some organisms over others. Dar-

[2] The American anthropologist Loren Eiseley credits Blyth, a British naturalist, with the early (1835 and 1837) formulation of the basic tenets of the theory of natural selection. Curiously, acknowledgment of this important contribution was conspicuously missing from Darwin's copious and detailed references to Blyth's work. For more on this thesis see Eiseley's article "Charles Darwin, Edward Blyth, and the Theory of Natural Selection," (*Proceedings of the American Philosophical Society*, Vol. 103, No. 1 [February, 1959], pp. 94–158). Be this as it may, Darwin did credit English naturalist A. R. Wallace (in a joint paper published by the Linnaean Society of London, 1858) with having independently reached the same general conclusion about evolution.

win expanded this basic idea of competition between populations into a theory entailing three generalizations: (a)
struggle for existence—borrowed from Malthus' discussion of
the consequences of intense competition for food; (b) *biological variation*—concluded from Darwin's own field observations that living things vary along numerous dimensions—
size, strength, intelligence, etc.—which provide the raw material for adaptation to a changing environment; (c) *natural
selection*, or survival of the fittest—a hypothetical position
which holds that an organism best endowed by nature to
satisfy its needs lives on to reproduce its kind. On this last
point, Darwin actually distinguished between *sexual selection* and ordinary natural selection—the former, he argued,
depends on success in competition among males for the at-
tentions of females, and on female choice (this being the
more important determinant); while natural selection arises
from the struggle to survive the many rigors of the environment in competition with other organisms of the same and
different kinds. The British zoologist C. B. Moffat (1903)
was among the earliest writers to disagree with Darwin,
suggesting that sexual selection could be attributed to the
more general case of natural selection. This view was more
fully expressed by the eminent biologist J. S. Huxley (1934).

Darwin disagreed with Lamarck as to the origin of new
species. Opposing the idea that differences produced during
an animal's own lifetime are transmitted to the offspring,
Darwin argued that the variations in body and organ forms
crop up in a chance manner, to be perpetuated or not, according to their adaptive value. Given enough of these
differences spread over periods of changing geography and
climate, one could account for the evolution of new species.
Of course, neither of these men knew about modern genetics
(i.e., mutation) as such and consequently harbored some
erroneous beliefs.

In later work Darwin applied his evolutionary theory to
the development of emotional and intellectual traits in ani-

mals. His *The Descent of Man* (1871) and *The Expression of the Emotions in Man and Animals* (1872) are significant landmarks in the history of comparative ethology. They are replete with examples of homologous (correspondence in type of structure and deriving from a common primitive source) and analogous (similarity in function but not in origin and structure) behavior in animals and man. For example, the sneer in man may be seen as a remnant of the animal's preparation to bite, the clenching of the fist a carry-over from the extension of the animal claw, etc. He also compared the mental powers of animals and humans, showing the presence of similar kinds of innate and acquired mechanisms in both groups such as imitation, curiosity, imagination and reasoning. In a sense, Darwin's research helped bridge the Cartesian schism between animal and human life. In any event, it certainly proved to be a great impetus to the study of comparative psychology.

C. Ramifications of Darwinian Theory— Early Animal Psychology

An interesting development in evolutionary theory, though not related to animal psychology as such, is English philosopher Herbert Spencer's general statement that evolution consists in a change from an "indefinite, incoherent homogeneity to a definite, coherent heterogeneity" (*Principles of Psychology*, 1855). According to this view, all phenomena, regardless of their nature—solar systems, embryos, or societies—are fashioned from agglomerations of matter into various integrated forms. The mind matures as a consequence of its coping with an ever-changing environment. In this sense, an animal's nervous system itself is adaptive; it passes from a simple, homogeneous state to a complex, differentiated state as it adapts to varying environmental conditions.

The most immediate effect of Darwin's doctrine of evolu-

tion was concern for the mentality of animals. English naturalist Douglas Spalding is usually credited with being the
first to apply the experimental method in animal psychology.
In 1873, one year after Darwin's important *Expression of the
Emotions in Man and Animals* appeared, Spalding published
the results of his experiments on instinctive behavior in birds.
In an attempt to determine the extent to which complicated
behavior could be accounted for in terms of pure instinct,
he confined newly hatched swallows to cages away from the
sight of other swallows until they reached flying age. Upon
their release, Spalding discovered that they could fly in the
absence of the customary experiences. In other experiments,
Spalding employed an ingenious procedure in which newly
hatched chicks were deprived of visual experiences by means
of little hoods (some opaque and others semitransparent)
placed over their heads and tied close around their necks.
Unhooding them one to three days later, he concluded that
pecking, involving the perception of direction and distance,
was an innate rather than a learned act. Other research
pointed to the importance of what now is known as *imprinting*—in Spalding's own words: "Chickens as soon as they are
able to walk will follow any moving object. And, when
guided by sight alone, they seem to have no more disposition
to follow a hen than to follow a duck, or a human being."
(*Instinct, With Original Observations on Young Animals*,
1873). Actually, recognition of this fact is to be found in
Thomas More's *Utopia* (1516): "[The chicks] are no sooner
out of the shell, and able to stir about, but they seem to
consider those that feed them as their mothers, and follow
them as other chickens do the hen that hatched them."

Following these pioneering studies came a series of fascinating observations on insects. Entomologists Jean Henri
Fabre in France (1885) and Sir John Lubbock in England
(1882) concerned themselves with the surprisingly advanced
behavior of ants, bees, wasps, and other insects. Although
their observations were carefully made and splendidly re-

corded, their conclusions served to exaggerate the uniformity in behavior at the expense of its variability. The marvels of Fabre's world are delightfully portrayed in his late publication, *The Wonders of Instinct: Chapters in the Psychology of Insects,* 1918. He was able to wed beauty of prose with the rigor of systematic observation and experiment. The feeding habits of the green grasshopper, the oak-worming of the larva of the capricorn beetle, the mortuary activities of the burying beetle (*Necrophorus*), and the egg-laying stratagems of the bluebottle are but a few samples of insect behavior which grace his enchanting book. Lubbock is also to be remembered for his contributions to laboratory methodology. He was probably the first to use "mazes" (Y-shaped, elevated, and multiple-unit varieties) in a systematic study of animal intelligence.

British biologist George Romanes wrote what is considered to be the first book on comparative psychology (*Animal Intelligence,* 1881). This book, although replete with anecdotal and anthropomorphic reasoning, supported the Darwinian thesis of continuity in the evolutionary development of animal life. In an attempt to establish a relationship between infrahuman and human mentality, Romanes proposed three kinds of ideational states and their prevalence in the animal kingdom: *simple ideas,* including sensory impressions, perceptions, and memories of past perceptions, all believed to be common to the entire range of animal life; *complex ideas,* encompassing various combinations of simple ideas, believed to be the province of some animals and all men; *notional ideas,* or abstractions and symbolic thinking, conceived of as unique prerogatives of most men. Related to this tripartite breakdown of mental life is Romanes' recapitulation theory of animal development. By means of anecdotal evidence he concluded that the mental status of the embryonic and early postnatal stages of humans compares closely to the mental levels of the various phyla of the animal kingdom. At birth, for example, the human is at the mental level of echinodermata (small sea animals), then, during the next fifteen months, twelve successively higher phyletic stages of development are recapitulated until the mental level of the dog and the anthropoid ape are approximated.

The anecdotal and anthropomorphic methods of Romanes were soon attacked by the more rigorous scientists. English zoologist Conwy Lloyd Morgan (1894), one of the strongest critics of the anecdotal school, proposed a means of avoiding the interpretive extravagances of Romanes in his famous canon: "In no case may we interpret an action as the outcome of the exercise of a higher psychical faculty, if it can be interpreted as the outcome of the exercise of one which stands lower in the psychological scale." [3] Besides the need for greater parsimony in science, Morgan called for greater control in techniques of observation, separation of interpretation from fact, and increased objectivity in reporting.

Morgan is also important for his experimental work in animal psychology. In addition to introducing (more explicitly than Bain had done) the "trial-and-practice" or *trial-and-error* concept of solving problems, he pursued research in much the same manner as did Lubbock, both engaging in systematic observations and controlled manipulations largely in natural environments. Working with several different animal species (e.g., chickens, ducks, and various kinds of rodents), Morgan sought to trace the development of behavior through its various stages. Crucial to this program was his use of the "incubation method," whereby chicks and ducklings were isolated for varying periods of time after hatching in hopes of distinguishing between innate and

---

[3] This is actually a special case of a celebrated statement by the English Franciscan theologian William of Ockham (or Occam). "Occam's razor" is often misquoted as *entia non sunt multiplicanda praeter necessitatem,* rather than what he actually wrote (1343): *pluralitas non est ponenda sine necessitate.* In any case, both exhort against assuming the existence of more, or more complex, entities than the least and simplest needed to explain facts (English ethologist S. A. Barnett suggests that a historical search be made for instances in which adherence to this principal of parsimony has actually led to error, i.e., a fallacious view of reality!)

learned behavior. Of particular significance in these genetic studies was Morgan's concept of *deferred instincts,* i.e., innate, complex, and stereotyped behavior that manifests itself after birth following a period of maturation.

As to theory, Morgan hypothesized three levels of mental activity somehow related to both ontogenetic and phylogenetic development. From an initial condition of vague consciousness, organisms are presumed to progress through a state characterized by the ability to form associations enroute to clear consciousness of the self. The final stage of self-awareness, Morgan asserted, is fundamental to the psychological process of imitation. Higher infrahuman animals, though capable of employing associated ideas in the solving of simple tasks, were considered bereft of true reason. Only man appeared fully capable of the last stage of development.

Extreme mechanistic interpretations of animal behavior found their spokesman in the person of German-born biophysiologist Jacques Loeb (1912). Using the methods of the botanist, he concluded that most, if not all, of the behavior of lower animals was *tropistic* (a turning to or away from specific stimuli, controlled purely by chemical and physical elements) in much the same way as that of plants, and therefore unconscious. For example, Loeb regarded the flight of moths into a flame as an automatic reaction to the relative amounts of irritation on different parts of the insects' body surface. He believed that there was a basic similarity between this type of behavior and, say, the heliotropism of certain plants involving the warming of one side of the stem by sunlight causing evaporation of moisture on that side and shrinking of tissue so that the plant bends in the direction of the sun. The "mechanomorphic" (a term used by Julian Huxley) school took firm hold, particularly in America and Russia.

Others extended Loeb's theories in developing a radical form of mechanistic behaviorism. A group of "German objectivists" (A. Bethe, T. Beer, J. von Uexküll, and others) introduced the language of biochemistry and biophysics in an attempt to describe animal behavior with complete objectivity. They proposed such new terms as *phonoreception* and *photoreception,* to describe a response to sound without referring to hearing and a reaction to light without referring to seeing. This endeavor, along with the proposals of other mechanists (e.g., J. P. Neul, who wanted to explain human behavior in the same way), intensified the mechanist-vitalist controversy. Consciousness, argued some mechanists, appears at a point in the phylogenetic scale characterized by the capacity for learned associations. Organisms unable to form these associations are presumably controlled completely by automatic mechanisms such as tropisms. This enabled the scientist to treat the question experimentally, provided that he could offer an acceptable definition of associative learning!

Among the more helpful critics of this period was American zoologist Herbert Spencer Jennings (1906), who urged moderation in the acceptance of the mechanistic position, primarily because of the great variability which he observed in the behavior of protozoa. Such behavior could not be described merely in terms of the customary physical and chemical formulae. Jennings insisted that the general nature of animal behavior be understood at a level of description fundamentally deterministic in nature, though different from that used by the physical scientist.

American psychologist Edward Lee Thorndike (1898) attempted a systematic study of the laboratory behavior of normal animals. Using the problem box as standard equipment, he made fish escape the sunlight by swimming through a specified exit in their tank, chicks learn to find their way out of mazes, and dogs, cats, and apes manipulate strings and bars to escape from their cages. In this manner, Thorndike was able to quantify rate of learning on the basis of correct and incorrect units of action performed and of time or number of trials taken to escape from the problem box. When plotted, these measurements provided evidence supporting the chance development of associations. Thorndike observed that the final successful act occurred more frequently than any of the various incorrect acts; consequently, the development of learning, he reasoned, is similar to the use and disuse of muscles, in that the action which is performed most often will become the readiest response (*Laws of Exercise and Readiness*). In addition to these postulates, Thorndike supported earlier views of Lloyd Morgan that animals will continue to perform those acts which are satisfying and discontinue those acts which lead to an annoying state of affairs (early *Law of Effect*). Additional research caused him to favor a truncated version of this law in which reward plays a more powerful and predictable role than punishment.

Of specific interest to comparative psychology is Thorndike's conclusion that the process of learning is essentially the same throughout the phylogenetic scale—i.e., learned associations are dependent on the number of possible neural connections which increase with phyletic development. Furthermore, an animal's capacity to learn is simply its ability to modify such connections (to break some and to develop others) as needs and circumstances dictate. Thus, differences in ability from species to species are basically differences of *degree* not of *kind* (i.e., they are quantitative, not qualitative), and that animals high in the phylogenetic scale possess nervous systems that afford *more* elements for development. Thorndike paid little attention to the neurophysiological aspects of the animal's brain, observing only that some brains allow for a greater number of neural connections than others. Here again the emphasis was on mechanomorphism—the implication being that animals and man are basically complex reflex machines.

Russian physiologist Ivan Pavlov (1890) provided the behaviorist with the extremely valuable research tool of *conditioning*. In brief, he discovered that a response which is customarily elicited by a given stimulus will result from a substitute stimulus provided that the latter is presented repeatedly just prior to the former. Although Pavlov worked with several types of conditioned reflexes, he relied upon the salivary response of the dog because the glands involved are normally not variable in their tonicity and so can be controlled. The salivary response was recorded by measuring the amount and rate of flow of saliva as it dropped from a catheter which had been inserted through the cheek of the dog into the appropriate glands. Pavlov found the time order in the presentation of stimuli to be a crucial variable; e.g., conditioning is difficult, if it occurs at all, if the stimulus to which the animal naturally responds is presented before the neutral stimulus (*backward conditioning*).

Pavlov left a rich body of methodology and basic data on conditioning. Of particular interest here is the use to which Pavlovian conditioning has been put by the animal psychologist. An animal's discriminatory abilities may be measured, for example, by conditioning it to respond to a given stimulus, say a certain tone, and then building up conditioned inhibitions (produced by allowing a response to occur in the absence of reinforcement) to tones that vary slightly from it. If an animal can learn to respond differently to any two auditory stimuli, it must be capable of distinguishing them. In this way, the animal reveals an aspect of its perceptual world in a language of behavior that meets with the rigorous standards of the scientist.

Although Pavlov's work was presented to American psychologists as early as 1909 by Yerkes and Morgulis, it wasn't until the research of Florence Mateer (1916) that Pavlovian conditioning took hold in the United States. Of these, psychobiologist Robert Yerkes was by far the most important person for our purposes. His research was primarily with primates, and to this end he helped establish the Yale Primate Laboratory (1927). One of his more important books was *The Great Apes: A Study of Anthropoid Behavior* (1929), which included, among other information, descriptions of their sensory capacities, their ability to perceive form, distance, and movement, their ability to learn, and their emotional life. His earlier research involved the use of the "multiple-choice" method (devised by Gilbert van T. Hamilton, 1911) in an attempt to rank different animals in order of learning ability. By this method, the animal is trained to distinguish from several possible alternatives the response which bears some particular relation to the other possible responses—for example, in the presence of several doorways the animal is required to learn to push open the first door to the left of whatever other door is standing open. Animals could be assigned "intelligence quotients," so to speak, on the basis of their success with problems of graded difficulty.

In an attempt to lend credence to the Lamarckian hypothesis of the inheritance of acquired characteristics, English-born William McDougall (1927) compared the ability of successive generations of rats to learn the correct avenue of escape from a tank of water. He found a significant improvement in the rate of learning within a span of sixteen generations. The bias of special selection (i.e., for those reactions favorable to training) could not be ruled out in McDougall's studies.[4] In any event, if patterns of behavior can be inherited, then it follows, reasoned McDougall, that the organization of the neuromuscular system, by which behavior is expressed, is in some way predetermined in the

[4] P. L. Broadhurst's "Behavioral Inheritance: Past and Present," *Conditional Reflex,* January–March, 1966, elaborates on this point. Apparently I. P. Pavlov at one time harbored a similar belief as the result of experiments by his student Studentsov (who found that successive generations of mice improved in the number of trials required to learn a particular conditioned response, 1923). McDougall and Rhine followed with several studies supporting the hypothesis of the inheritance of acquired characteristics, or, as Broadhurst puts it, "the transformation of [acquired] conditioned responses into [innate] unconditioned ones." As indicated above, the positive results were thought to be due to some unconscious selection of the test animals. Be this as it may, convincing refutation of the Lamarckian view was exhaustively given in a series of experiments by F. A. E. Crew (1936), W. E. Agar, F. H. Drummond and O. W. Tiegs (1935–1954).

germ cell. American biologist Ross Harrison (1904) had provided partial support for this belief by showing that frog embryos raised in a chloroform solution developed functional reflexes in much the same way as those embryos raised normally.

But this was not the full story. Other investigators reported that embryonic development of behavior was affected by certain immediate environmental factors in a way that precludes hereditary influence. American zoologist S. R. Detwiler (1922), for example, found that budding limbs of frog and salamander embryos transplanted to other parts of the animals' bodies (even to the tops of their heads) grow into legs that function in quite a normal manner. It was discovered that the limb buds stimulate the growth of nerve fiber toward their altered location contrary to the usual direction of growth determined by heredity.

Unlike Detwiler, who observed experimentally induced behavior, behaviorist Z-Y. Kuo (1932) concentrated on the development of the chick embryo in a natural environment. By removing a portion of the eggshell and oiling the protecting membrane to make it transparent, he was able to observe the natural growth of chick embryos. Most significant of his findings was the relationship between the pulsation of the thoracic artery against which the head rested and the rhythmic movement of the head. This rhythmic movement appeared to develop into postnatal pecking behavior.[5]

Such studies underscore the significance of environmental influences on the structural and functional development of the individual organism. Taken together with the investiga-

[5] Konrad Lorenz, the eminent Austrian animal behaviorist, questions this conclusion; he points out that "only certain birds peck after hatching, while others gape like passerines, dabble like ducks, or shove their bills into the corner of the mouth of the parents as pigeons do, although they all, when embryos, had their heads moved up and down by the heartbeat in exactly the same fashion" (*Evolution and Modification of Behavior,* 1965). Kuo replies in his new book, *The Dynamics of Behavior Development; An Epigenetic View,* 1967. See Appendix B for a discussion of the ethologist's approach to instinct and animal behavior.

tions showing the importance of constitutional factors, we see the relevance of Leonard Carmichael's statement (1926): "Heredity and environment are not antithetical, nor can they expediently be separated."

IX. Early European Functional Psychology: The Minds of Men

> Nature never rhymes her children, nor
> makes two men alike.
>
> R. W. EMERSON

A. Differential Psychology and Statistics— Individual Differences

The study of individual differences came into its own with the efforts of Sir Francis Galton (1869). The famous Englishman's work was not without precedents. Plato had recognized differing abilities among men in the organization of education and delegation of duties in the ideal state; Quintilian, the first-century A.D. Roman rhetorician, wrote convincingly on individual variation in ability and the need for remedial education in cases of dullness; Brown's secondary laws of association included the factor of constitutional differences; Herbart had considered intelligence as a variable in the development of associations; Bessel had found a wide variation in the speed of response among his fellow astronomers; Weber, Fechner, Helmholtz and Wundt had also noted individual differences among their subjects, but failed to study them systematically. Granting such exceptions, most philosophers and psychologists before Galton had been concerned primarily with mind in its *nomothetic* (universal) rather than its *idiographic* (unique) sense. Galton was unquestionably the first to undertake a systematic and statistical study of individual psychology.

Basic to Galton's investigations was the supposition that individual differences among persons result primarily from hereditary factors. Men inherited not only genius or, by implication, stupidity but also specific forms of each. The eminent musicians come from a pedigree of great musicians just as certainly as severe moronity stems from a defective family line. Such traits as criminality were also believed to be inherited, and this Galton supposedly substantiated by anthropometric studies of the "criminal type." The Italian psychiatrist-anthropologist, Cesare Lombroso (1876), later extended this idea, offering an inverted evolutionary hypothesis of the *atavistic* habitual criminal—i.e., mental and physical reversion to primitive savagery.

As to contributions in methodology, Galton developed tests for the measurement of psychological differences, and also statistical procedures for the analysis of such data. In research on mental association, he determined both the time required to arouse associations following some word or signal and the actual response made. Responses could be in the form of gestures (usually first to occur), verbal associations (next to occur), and finally concrete images. Galton expanded his research on *mental imagery* by means of the questionnaire method. This method, used so extensively in psychological research for the first time, enabled Galton to quantify images into serial order from low to high intensity. He found marked differences in the amount and vividness of imagery among different people, and also within the same person at different times. "Number forms," a phenomenon akin to *synesthesia* (the general term used for situations in which a stimulus to one sense modality arouses a definite feeling in another modality) was alluded to in this fashion. Strength of imagery and cases of synesthesia were found to run in families just as did intelligence or criminality.

In further probes into the nature of individual differences, Galton collected anecdotal reports on identical twins showing gross similarities in their life history of physical development, disease, mental capacity, etc., irrespective of their environmental backgrounds. Although little was known about the mechanics of heredity, Galton advanced the idea of *eugenics,* in which the primary aim was the systematic improvement of the race through the study and implementation of biological laws.[1] In this effort, he not only developed standards of human ability upon which to base eugenic principles but also established an anthropometric laboratory, located for the longest period at the South Kensington Museum in London. Various instruments were provided on a table along one side of a narrow room through which people passed, guided by the superintendent, who filled in data as each person tested his strength of pull and squeeze, breathing power, quickness of punch, hearing, vision, color sense, etc. Galton's ultimate goal was to determine the mental resources in Great Britain by subjecting all its inhabitants to his battery of sensory discrimination tests. An ambitious program indeed and Galton was confronted with the practical problem of boiling down these data.[2] Toward this end, he ingeniously extended the statistical theorizing of the Belgian astronomer, Lambert Quetelet (1835) in an attempt to present a quantitative summary of large masses of data. Where Quetelet had concentrated on applying the theory of the normal probability curve to the interpretation of biological and social data, Galton's single greatest contribution to quantitative psychology was the invention of the rudiments of correlation. In the hands of capable mathematicians such as Englishman Karl Pearson (1897), this simple though heuristic device for measuring concomitant variation grew into more advanced methods for ascertaining the reliability

[1] Galton knew of Darwin's theory of *pangenesis* (that every element of the organism gives forth diminutive hereditary particles, or *gemmules,* representative of its characters, present in the body at large and also stored in the reproductive cells to be passed on to the progeny), and he experimented with blood transfusions between different strains of rabbits toward the development of a more sophisticated genetic theory that was quite advanced for the period.

[2] He actually collected data on 9,337 people during the existence of the laboratory. Although no significant generalizations resulted, it did represent a dramatic pioneering effort in the study of human individual differences. Galton was interested also in testing the sensory capacities of animals, and to this end he invented several gadgets, the best known of which was the "Galton whistle."

and validity of tests, in addition to the various factor analytic techniques. The symbol for the coefficient of correlation, r, taken from the first letter of "regression," serves to commemorate, somewhat obliquely, Galton's discovery that inherited characteristics tend to *regress* toward the mean of a distribution of those characteristics.

The founding of the journal *Biometrika* (1901) by Galton, Pearson and W. F. R. Weldon attests to the gaining importance of statistical methods in the biological and psychological sciences of that period.

The mental testing movement was advanced immeasurably by the early twentieth-century research of French psychologists Alfred Binet [3] and Théodore Simon (1905). Appointed by the French government to the task of assessing the intellectual level of French school children (for the purpose of separating the subnormal children for special education), Binet and Simon prepared a set of tasks divided into graduated levels of difficulty. Unlike the simple sensory-motor tasks devised by Galton, the Binet-Simon battery was predicated on a theory of intelligence entailing concepts of goal direction, adaptability, and critical judgment. The tests themselves consisted of items of common information, word definition, symbol recall, simple reasoning, ingenuity, and the like. In administering these tests to large numbers of children, they were able to arrange individual problems on a scale of difficulty by locating each at a point where a majority (50 to 75 per cent) of the children of a given age gave correct answers. With graded items of this sort an individual's

---

[3] Of interest to the author is the fact that Binet wrote the first book on the psychology of chess (*Psychologie des grande calculateurs et des joueurs d'Echecs*, 1894). Studying the psychological faculties of blindfolded chess players, Binet concluded that the ability to play blindfolded rests on three fundamental conditions: knowledge and experience in the field of chess (*l'érudition*), imagination (*l'imagination*) and memory (*la mémoire*). A critical appraisal of Binet's thesis along with a wealth of other materal on this subject are to be found in Dutch psychologist Adriaan D. de Groot's *Thought and Choice in Chess*, 1965.

mental age was given simply by designating how far along the scale of difficulty he could manage.

Thus, the two French investigators initiated a major breakthrough in the area of mental testing. Although many others were to follow, it is fitting to choose the English psychologist Charles Spearman for special mention, since his two-factor theory of intellectual ability actually antedated the work of Binet and Simon by one year (1904).[4] A basic assumption in Spearman's mathematical approach to intelligence (similar to Galton) is that all mental tasks require both *general* and *specific* abilities. The former, *G*, derived from a "hierarchy of intercorrelations," is believed to be common to all intellectual problems, whereas *s* is specific to a given task. So we may have some individuals exhibiting a high general level of intellectual performance, and others a moderate or even low general level combined with an above-average functioning in one or more special areas.

B. *Social Psychology—Its Basic Nature*

Psychology in the seventeenth and eighteenth centuries thrived on simple, unitary explanations of social behavior. Thomas Hobbes, the English philosopher, believed that man is basically egotistical; all social behavior was interpreted as the direct or disguised result of individual power seeking. Socialization is possible only through man's submission to the "common power" of the state—or as expressed in Hobbes's *Leviathan* (1651), recognition of the supreme authority of

[4] American psychologists Chaplin and Krawiec (*Systems and Theories of Psychology*, 1960) point out that Spearman's theory did not gain prominence until the mental-testing program had been given impetus by the early development of intelligence tests. Once it did take hold, it not only provided theoretical grist for international controversy but also became the starting point for rival theories of intelligence. G. H. Thomson at Edinburgh (sampling theory, 1930) and L. L. Thurstone at Chicago (weighted group-factor theory, 1935) offered two such rival theories.

the sovereign—and engagement in a social contract to obtain protection from other power-seeking mortals. Only in this way can man find time to participate in the nonmilitant pursuits of learning, recreation and religion. Variants of this view, that social organization better enables man to realize his selfish interests, are manifest in the philosophy of German Friedrich Nietzsche (1885) and in the psychiatry of Austrian Alfred Adler (1918), to mention just two more recent examples.

Related to Hobbes's emphasis on selfishness is English jurist Jeremy Bentham's discourse on ethical *hedonism* (1789). Of social psychological importance here is Bentham's insistence that men act so as to maximize the pleasure of others in the pursuit of self-gratification. Furthermore, the policy of all social agencies should be to facilitate "the greatest happiness of the greatest number." This can best be done, argued Bentham, by a laissez-faire, or hands-off, governmental policy.

In opposition to the egocentric theories of social behavior are the equally parsimonious views of such men as French psychologist Théodule Ribot (sympathy is "the foundation of all social existence"), Russian philosopher Peter Kropotkin (instinct of "human solidarity" as the cornerstone of society), and French sociologist Gabriel Tarde ("society is imitation"). Most important of these men for the history of social psychology is Tarde, who probably wrote the first modern work in the field (*Les Lois de l'imitation*, 1890). Three laws of imitation were expounded: (a) the imitation of the socially superior by the socially inferior (*law of descent*); (b) the rapid spread of fashion, rumor, and craze from the point of origin (*law of geometrical progression*); (c) the preference for imitating one's own culture over another (*law of internal before the exotic*). Beyond the exposition of these laws, Tarde had little concrete to say about the actual process of imitation as it applies to social behavior, except that it was characterized in many cases by increased suggestibility.

An interesting ramification of Tarde's theorizing is seen in Gustave Le Bon's concen for the relationship between suggestion and crowd behavior (*The Crowd*, 1895). The French physician and sociologist wrote of a discrete group or crowd mentality emerging from the interaction of individual minds. This conception of social behavior is essentially Hegelian in spirit. For Hegel (1807), the state was conceived of as a transcendent Mind, an absolute, all-embracing, divine reality; individual men are but agents, and the state although made up of individuals is in no way reducible to their transitory mental lives. Other social philosophers interpreted matters in much the same way: German political philosopher Karl Marx conceived of social class as a supraindividual entity; Thomas Hill Green, a nineteenth-century English idealist philosopher, depicted the state as an organic mind transcending the component minds of individuals; Wilhelm Wundt and French sociologist Émile Durkheim also entertained the notion that associations among humans produce thoughts, manners, and practices which are external to, and independent of, any single individual. Needless to say, the concept of *group mind* was severely criticized on grounds of invoking quasi-supernatural constructs to account for natural, albeit complicated, phenomena. American psychologist Floyd Allport (1924), for example, argued that one can still talk about individuals and their interactions as being something more than mere summation, and yet not a separate entity.

Of perhaps greatest significance in these early years of social psychology was the impressive theorizing of William McDougall (1908). Borrowing heavily from evolutionary theory, McDougall built a completely coherent system of social psychology around the concept of instinct. Central to his definition of instinct are three primary characteristics, all conceived of as innate psychophysical dispositions: (a) a perceptual or *cognitive* aspect which induces the organism to perceive certain situations in a specific way; (b) an emotional or *affective* aspect pertaining to a body state appropriate to what is perceived; (c) a striving or *conative* aspect involving a *purposeful* action, or impulse to action, in accordance with the emotion engendered by a particular perception. This last characteristic of the purposive, the striving-toward-a-goal nature of instinctive behavior is actually the essence of McDougall's entire psychological system (sometimes referred to as *hormic*, or "impulse," psychology). McDougall allowed for considerable modifiability at the ends of his tripartite system—i.e., both stimulus (cognitive) and response (conative) characteristics are subject to change, due to varying environmental contingencies. The truly immutable nature of instinct was believed to be in the emotional or affective phase, so that any stimulus triggering an affective state may vary somewhat with learning, but the emotion itself persists unchanged.

If one disregards McDougall's attempts at cataloguing human instincts, there is an impressive degree of sophistication in his theoretical discussions on innate social behavior. The same can be said of William James's speculations on instinctive behavior; both of these men explicitly or implicitly anticipated some of the more cogent notions of contemporary ethology, as we shall see later in this book. Be this as it may, the views of McDougall, James, and others attempting to apply instinct theory to social psychology (e.g., John Dewey, Wilfred Trotter, Robert Woodworth) fell into disrepute at the hands of critics such as Dunlap and Bernard.

Knight Dunlap (1919) is credited with hurling the first "anti-instinct" bombshell. He accused McDougall of unjustly ascribing purpose to all instinctive acts. Is it possible, argued Dunlap, that purpose guides every impulsive act of animals or very young children? An affirmative answer to this question of teleology hardly seemed to comply with the law of parsimony in light of the biological knowledge at hand. Anti-instinct criticism was rampant in the following ten years. Luther Bernard (1926), among others, maintained that the term *instinct* had become the catch-all for all types of uniformity in human social behavior. One has only to scan the then published lists of so-called social instincts to understand Bernard's objection to such *ad hoc* and unrestrained proliferation.

Historian Gardner Murphy points out that the effectiveness of the anti-instinct revolt left social psychology toward the end of the twenties devoid of any generally acceptable theoretical basis. Without a unifying theory of any kind social psychologists had little choice but to adopt a fresh, more empirical approach toward alternative conceptions of human nature.

C. *Developmental Psychology—The Formative Years*

As indicated earlier in this book, Herbart's concept of apperceptive mass is viewed in relation to the developing organism. The rather obvious point that what one already knows affects the assimilation of new material has had the most extraordinary influence on developmental (including both child and educational) psychology. But Herbart's idea, as applied to the maturing human organism, was more the culmination of work by Rousseau, Pestalozzi, and Froebel than the launching of something new.

The Swiss-born social philosopher, Jean Jacques Rousseau (1762) advocated that education of children be directed toward the development of their natural or inherent capacities. In his treatise on education (*Émile*) we read:

Each child has his own cast of mind, in accordance with which he must be directed; and if we would succeed, he must be ruled according to his natural bent and no other. Be judicious; watch nature long, and observe your pupil carefully before you say a word to him. At least leave the germ of his character free to disclose itself. Repress it as little as possible, so that you may the better see all there is of it.

This view was consistent with Rousseau's metaphysical assumption of the unspoiled nature of primitive man and the corrupting influences of civilization. "God made all things good; man meddles with them and they become evil"—and so the romantic fallacy of the *noble savage* was born.

Another Swiss educational reformer, Johann Pestalozzi (1781), concerned himself with the actual pedagogical techniques to be used in sensitizing the callow learner to the diversity of his surroundings. Consistent with Rousseau's philosophy, children were taught to observe with care the various things they encountered in the classroom, at home, and in the field. Pestalozzi believed that concrete observations of this sort would better equip the child to adjust to the ever-increasing complexities of adult life. In professing basically the same philosophy, although differing with Pestalozzi as to method, educator Friedrich Froebel (1836) emphasized the educational value of play as a means of allowing for the natural development of the child. To this end, the German educational reformer founded the *Kindergarten* in which preschool children could participate in supervised play with, *inter alia*, attractively colored toys to develop their capacities for dealing with things.

Somewhat later, and under the direct influence of both Herbart and Fechner, the German physiologist Wilhelm Preyer wrote *Die Seele des Kindes* (*The Mind of the Child*, 1882) which probably represents the first systematic study in developmental psychology. His book, for the most part, consists of a compilation of childhood instincts and reflexes relating to the behaviors of imitation, intellectual and emotional expressions, etc. It was actually psychologist G. Stanley Hall (1904) who greatly expanded the scope of developmental psychology, but since he was an American, discussion of his contributions will be held in abeyance until we cross the Atlantic in the following chapter.

One last person to be discussed in the present context is still another famous Swiss psychologist, Jean Piaget. While

Professor Piaget is very much alive today, his psychological researches began in the early 1920s. (Actually Piaget had published twenty papers on molluscs and similar species before this period.) Though a "functionalist" at heart, Piaget departed substantially not only from his Swiss predecessor Édouard Claparède, but also from the whole of the traditional European school of psychology, in offering lucid examples of the means by which young children come to comprehend their physical and social environments. Most important, from a methodological point of view, is his imaginative use of the *méthode clinique* as a semistandardized device for testing cognitive development in children. Working with subjects (including his own children) between the ages of two and fifteen years, Piaget and his many colleagues have delved into real-life problems, such as the development of the child's conceptions of reality, of causality, of number, and of social norms and morality. By means of clinical interview they found that intellectual development in the small child proceeds from an uncomplicated egocentric mode of thought through stages marked by gradual cognitive emancipation enroute to the pre-adolescent period of logical thinking. In all of this work, Piaget and his students (sometimes called the Geneva group) emphasize the invariance of the *sequence* of stages, not the exact age at which a given stage is achieved. This means that in some cultures the development through certain stages is retarded or accelerated depending on various circumstances, but the sequence is believed to be everywhere the same.

As an example of the developmental stages the thinking of a child is presumed to follow, we might look at Piaget's research on moral judgment (*The Moral Judgment of the Child*, 1932). The Swiss or French child of two or three plays marbles with great exuberance; his delight appears to stem from a mixture of fantasy and sheer bodily movement, with no apparent concern for the "rules." When asked who won, the youngster is likely to answer, "I won, Ralph won, we all won!" From these early *autistic* contacts with the world, the child of four to six begins to conceive of rules as such, of fairness, and of scoring. Procedures of this sort become *absolute*, and departures from them are seen by the child as unmitigated infractions.[5] Things must be done exactly according to Hoyle or the play is not fair. Later, beginning at seven or eight years of age, rigidity over rules gives way to a more permissive attitude whereby the group to which the individual is a member may have the right to modify the procedures *relative* to its own needs. And finally, toward adolescence, the child comes to tolerate more drastic compromises in regulations, compensating in his eyes, as it were, for any inequities among the participants, such as physical handicaps.

More recent work (1950s) of the Geneva group divides general intellectual development into four main stages, each with several substages: the *sensorimotor* stage (birth to 2 or 3 years—from a body-centered world to an object-centered one); the *preoperational* stage (2 or 3 years to around 7 years—period when language is learned, permitting the child to manipulate his world symbolically); the stage of *concrete operations* (6 or 7 years to 11 or 12 years—transition from dependence on one's own perceptions and motor actions to the capacity for simple reasoning); and finally the stage of *formal operations* (11 or 12 years to 14 or 15 years—period when the child can deal with abstract relationships and the hypothetical instead of concrete objects). In a practical

[5] Maria Montessori, the well-known Italian physician and educator, relates an interesting story pertaining to this point and bearing on what she chooses to call the child's *love of order*. In playing hide-and-seek with three-year-old Italian children, she hid in a place different from that used by the others. The children, upon not finding her in their customary hiding place ("behind the door where you were supposed to be") refused to search elsewhere and became downcast over the departure in procedures laid down so explicitly beforehand. To quote Madame Montessori, "To hide something means for them to put it somewhere out of sight, where its rediscovery brings a sense of order not only in what can be seen but in what cannot be seen, so that they can say to themselves, 'You can't see it, but I know where it is, I can find something with my eyes shut, be sure of the place where it has been put.' " (*The Secret of Childhood*, 1936.)

sense, all of this suggests that the most effective methods of education will be those that are attuned to the style of thought which is natural to children of the age concerned. X

Piaget draws an interesting parallel between the development of cognitive thought in the child and the evolution of human knowledge. Ontogenetic processes in the development of, say, a child's conception of reality recapitulate the evolution in epistemology. In *The Child's Conceptions of Physical Causality*, 1930, Piaget states: ". . . the elimination of realism, of substantialism [bodies are born of one another but are no longer endowed with growth—e.g., clouds come from smoke but cannot grow], of dynamism [attributing force to objects, but without the implication that they are alive—e.g., the clouds move by themselves],[6] the growth of relativism, etc., all are evolutionary laws which appear to be common both to the development of the child and to that of scientific thought." It has been said that Piaget's main concern has been to establish such relationships in mathematical terms.

As is true of many innovators in science, the work of Piaget is subject to criticism from several camps: the rigorous methodologist complains of his ambiguous use of terms and the sometimes unreplicable clinical procedures; the theoretician finds fault with his underlying assumptions, such as the belief that "true" (i.e., biological) stages of development are being tapped rather than learned responses to specific cultural stimuli. And, of course, support for and against such assumptions has been offered by social scientists working with children from diverse cultural backgrounds: for example, children of the southwest Pacific show little, if any, autistic or animistic thinking (Margaret Mead); a study of certain American Indian tribes provides evidence confirming Piaget's belief in the biological basis of developmental stages in cognition (Wayne Dennis); and, less controversial, stages

[6] Specific definitions and examples in brackets were taken from J. P. Chaplin and T. S. Krawiec, *Systems and Theories of Psychology*, 1960.

in the development of spatial concepts are attained somewhat more slowly by Zulu children than by white children
in Africa (J. J. Cowley and M. Murray). Even though the
exact nature of these stages and the influences upon them
remain a moot question today, Piaget's contributions to developmental psychology are among the most insightful in
the field.

X. Early American Psychology: Development of an Old and a New System

> *... it is indeed true that problems are solved only where they arise—namely, in action, in the adjustment of behavior. But, for good or for evil, they can be solved there only with method; and ultimately method is intelligence, and intelligence is method.*
>
> JOHN DEWEY

A. German Content Psychology in America— Titchenerian Structuralism

The hard core of Wundt's psychological system migrated to America in the person of Edward Titchener (1898). Born and schooled in England, Titchener came under the influence of Wundt first through his books (translating into English Wundt's third and fourth editions of *Physiologische Psychologie*) and later as a graduate student at Leipzig from 1890 to 1892. Wundt made an indelible impression upon the younger man—one which was manifest throughout Titchener's next thirty-five years in America, where he replaced Frank Angell, another of Wundt's students, as director of the newly founded psychological laboratory at Cornell University.

Titchener's role in American psychology was unusual, to say the least. As the main expositor of Wundtian psychology, he was hardly sympathetic with aptitude testing, mental hygiene, and similar applied considerations, which commanded the interest of most American psychologists of the period. It is no wonder that Titchener remained aloof from American psychology in his capacities as theoretician and as researcher. Only a nominal member of the American Psychological Association from its inception in the early 1890s, Titchener left the organization in 1904 and established an informal group known as "Experimental Psychologists," which met yearly throughout the lifetime of its founder. The group was committed to the advancement of psychology as Wundt had preordained—a science restricted to the discovery of the laws governing the normal human mind; it was neither the vagaries of individual differences nor the superficialities of application, but the *generalized mind,* which deserved the serious research efforts of the experimental psychologist.

The subject matter of all science is experience, and for psychology it is experience *dependent* upon the experiencing person. It is imperative, argued Titchener, that experimental psychology be restricted, at least for the present, to a description of the mental *structure* underlying this experience in a manner similar to the taxonomic concerns of the anatomist rather than the functionalism of the physiologist. One effort leads to the meaningful and unequivocal compendium of mental elements, while the other, because it is premature, risks the dangers inherent in teleological and animistic description.

For Titchener the fundamental problem in psychology is to discover the *what* and *how* of mental structure. "What" is a question of analysis, i.e., the breakdown of consciousness to its constituent parts; "How" is a question of synthesis, i.e., ascertaining the laws governing the arrangement and combination of mental elements into conscious events as man experiences them. The question "Why" (especially as it relates to the *purpose* of consciousness) was, on the whole, outside the range of Titchener's concerns.[1]

[1] Although Titchener did concern himself somewhat with the causes of consciousness, his psychophysical parallelism did not allow for any direct connections between mind and body; nor did it imply either that the nervous system is fundamental to consciousness or that it is in any way more real than its mental counterpart. However, even though knowledge of the nervous system adds nothing unique, it is sometimes preferred in explanation because it is more continuous and less erratic than the perceptual world revealed through introspection.

As to the actual superstructure of the system, Titchener borrowed heavily from Wundt in postulating the existence of three fundamental elements of consciousness: *sensations, images,* and *feelings.* Sensations are the characteristic features of perception—i.e., the sights, sounds, smells, etc.— arising from sensory stimulation. Images are the characteristic features of ideas, and thus represent experiences not actually present to the individual. Feelings or affections are the elemental characteristics of emotion. All three classes of elements possess inseparable though variable "attributes" of *quality, intensity, extensity, duration, clearness* and possibly *vividness.* Elements and their attendant attributes comprise the basic units of psychic structure. Titchener used simple geometrical models to represent the exact relationships existing between sensory elements and their attributes. Ebbinghaus' "color pyramid" (relations between hue, saturation, and brightness of colors, 1893), Hans Henning's "olfactory prism" (relations between principal odors—burned, ethereal, fragrant, putrid, resinous and spicy—and their correspondence to specific organic chemicals, 1915) and "taste tetrahedron" (relations between the elementary taste qualities— salt, sour, sweet and bitter—and their dependence upon distinct types of organic chemicals, 1916), and Titchener's own "tonal pencil" (association of low tones with bigness and high tones with smallness) and "touch pyramid" (relations among the numerous discrete types of cutaneous sensations ascertained by means of trained introspection) are examples of such models. They all served to illustrate the elemental nature of sensations and their attributes. Images and their attributes are, in turn, subject to analysis in similar manner.

Special mention is needed of Titchener's views on feeling; it will be remembered from the earlier discussion of Wundt's tridimensional theory of feeling that those views were in sharp contrast to the beliefs of other structuralists. For Titchener, feeling is experienced as being pleasant or unpleasant, each to be thought of as a conscious element amenable to the same introspective analysis as are conscious properties of sensory elements. Feelings supposedly differ from sensations in that they are introspectively unlocalizable, have no attribute of intensity, do not occur independently (i.e., are always part of a sensation), and wane with repeated experience (while sensations adjust to continuous stimulation). Attempts by Wundt and his students to expand on the elemental make-up of feeling were discredited by Titchener as specious reasoning stemming from loose introspective techniques (e.g., committing the *stimulus error*, or interpreting rather than describing mental events). He argued that unlike the dimension of pleasantness-unpleasantness, strain-relaxation and excitement-depression (the remaining dimensions of Wundt's tripartite theory of feeling) are not true opposites. Relaxation, for example, is the absence of tension, not its opposite; and calm is the more logical opposite of excitement than is depression. Titchener preferred to call such experiences "muscular attitudes" rather than simple, elementary feelings.

The associationistic side of structuralism is seen best in Titchener's *context theory of meaning* (1910). In brief, it states that the meaning of any selected group of sensations (i.e., a perception) or images (i.e., an idea) is carried by the existing context of other sensations or images present in the mind. To this traditional brand of associationism, Titchener added the interesting principle that in familiar perceptions or ideas conscious context subsides so that meaning exists unconsciously. By so incorporating unconscious states, Titchener had accepted the validity of Ach's concept of determining tendecy (at least in matters of meaning) and Helmholtz's principle of unconscious inference.

B. *Beginnings of American Functionalism—*
A Break with Tradition

The change of scene from Europe to America was hardly a significant factor in Titchener's case. His close ties with Wundtian psychology insulated him from the pragmatically oriented *Platzgeist* (spirit of the place) of America. Why had American psychology chosen this course rather than pursue the analysis of consciousness as prescribed by Wundt? Many American psychologists had, in fact, studied at Leipzig under Wundt and had come away stanch experimentalists. But they returned to a land which in spirit was more conducive to evolutionary theory than any other country. Edwin Boring elaborates on this thesis, suggesting that America, as a pioneering country, accepted as a natural consequence of life the view that adaptation to environmental changes was the key to survival in the new world. A more staid England, for example, provided its intellectuals with the leisure for scientific contemplation and discovery, while the exigencies of life in a new land cried out for more practical considerations.

William James (1890) was one of the most influential forces in American psychology. Twenty-five years Titchener's senior, James had made significant headway in psychology long before structuralism (a Jamesian term) took hold at Cornell. In 1875 James introduced the rigors of experimentalism to his psychology students at Harvard University. German influences were apparent during this early period as shown by his frequent mention of the research of men such as Helmholtz and Wundt, and an invitation to the able German experimental psychologist Hugo Münsterberg to join the faculty at Harvard. Münsterberg left for the United States the same year Titchener joined Cornell, in 1892. He was well received and eventually was given a permanent professorship in psychology. James was particularly interested in Münsterberg's ingenious *action theory* (1900), which states that the degree of consciousness depends not on the excitation of some sensory area of the brain (as believed by the structuralists), but on the facility of nervous discharge from sense organ to motor response. In short, consciousness results from the completion of a receptor-effector circuit, and the more open the circuit, the more conscious the mental process accompanying it. This supposition appealed to James—it was attuned to the functionalistic belief that all life is impulsive and tends toward action.[2]

James was as inclusive and unsystematic in his approach to psychology as Titchener was exclusive and systematic. Problems having to do with individual differences and abnormal, comparative, and applied psychology were all grist for his mill. His more important contributions are set forth in two volumes of *The Principles of Psychology*, which, as historian Gardner Murphy writes, burst upon the world like a volcanic eruption. James wrote with the eloquence and verve of a first-rate novelist. This, coupled with a brilliant, erudite mind, made James America's foremost psychologist.

The starting point of human psychology for James is immediately felt experience, i.e., experience as man knows it firsthand. Such experience could best be described as a *stream of consciousness*, and any attempt to analyze it into discrete components was unwarranted. Persistence in such a futile enterprise leads one to commit the *psychologist's fallacy*, the assumption that when a mental complex has been reduced

---

[2] There were serious objections to the action theory. Margaret Washburn, Titchener's first doctoral candidate at Cornell (1916), maintained that a certain degree of resistance or blocking of motor nerve pathways intensifies rather than diminishes one's awareness of an event, e.g., although transmission of an impulse becomes easier and easier with the acquisition of a habit, consciousness of the behavior involved may decrease steadily. Taking a more critical position, William Montague (1908) suggested that there is an *inverse* rather than a direct relationship between openness of receptor-effector pathways and consciousness. Reflex action, for example, is an obvious case of an "open" sensory-motor circuit which can hardly be described as involving clear consciousness.

to parts, the parts must have been there all the time and are the essence of the complex. This was a direct criticism of the structuralist's use of trained introspection to tease out the supposed elements of the conscious mind.

The stream of consciousness has several characteristics: it is *personal* (thoughts belong to individuals and not to some abstract generalized mind); it is in *constant flux* (like Heraclitus' cosmology, one never experiences the same thought, idea, or feeling twice, since it is received against an ever-changing mental background); it is sensibly *continuous* (there exist no natural breaks in the stream, but an experienced continuity which waxes and wanes in intensity and rate of change); it is constantly *selective* (although the mental stream is replete with content, it attends to only a small portion at any given moment). James thought it important that psychologists confront what he called *transitive* as well as *substantive* states. The former arise as a consequence of the rapidly changing stream of thought; consciousness of this kind is not readily amenable to introspection because of its vague and incoherent nature. The imageless thoughts and determining tendencies of the Würzburg school might well be subsumed under James's broader category of transitive states.

James speculated creatively about the self, which he treats not as an abstraction but as a perceived reality. He differentiates three forms of the self: (a) *material self* (the body and all the physical possessions one can call his own); (b) *social self* or *selves* (in anticipation of more modern social role theory, James conceived of man as having as many social selves as he has roles to play in society); (c) *spiritual self* (the core self consisting of intellectual capacities, sensibilities, and will, or as James writes "all the psychic faculties or dispositions taken together"). A combination of these constitute the *empirical self*. Unity often does not prevail, and when there is a serious breakdown the resulting conflict among the various selves may produce personality dissociation or the severing and isolation of certain mental processes from the main stream of consciousness.

Another topic of considerable importance to James was that of emotion. In essence, emotion is seen as visceral activity which is reflexively aroused by certain situations.[3] James argued rather cogently that his theory ran counter to the common-sense notion which interpolates emotional reaction between the exciting stimulus and the bodily response. According to his view, rather than perceiving, emoting, and acting, one perceives, acts, and then emotes. In its support, James cites the apparent fact that one must assume characteristic postures to experience certain emotions; e.g., in a situation calling for exuberance, if instead of holding one's head high and chest out a slumping posture is assumed, no experience of exuberance will result. Two main criticisms of this theory came from Titchener, who insisted that James was confusing affection and organic sensation (which introspective analysis showed to be different phenomena), and from the physiologists Sir Charles Sherrington (1906) and Walter Cannon (1915), who found that animals whose spinal tracts had been severed at the neck still behaved in an emotional way to appropriate stimulation, even though most body sensations were eliminated.[4]

The breadth of James's professional interests knew few limits. In *The Varieties of Religious Experience* (1902), he first takes to task those who dismiss religious experience as

[3] It is noteworthy that French philosophers Descartes (1650) and Nicholas Malebranche (1674), and finally Danish physician Carl Lange (1885) held similar views. James and Lange's views were offered independently and differ in that the former emphasized visceral changes while the latter stressed circulatory activity (vasomotor disturbances) as the basis for emotions.

[4] Cannon and his student Philip Bard suggested a *thalamic theory*, which states that emotional experience and bodily changes are independent of each other, but that both are dependent upon the discharge from the hypothalamus. Tracing the process, emotion-provoking stimuli excite the hypothalamus, which in turn excites the cortex, viscera, and skeletal musculature simultaneously. Seen in this light, the experienced affect actually precedes bodily changes, since the cortex is more proximal to the hypothalamus than is the viscera.

valueless because of the supposed high incidence of mental abnormality among religious leaders, and then proceeds to define and describe not only religious experiences but varieties of mysticism as well. Mental stability, argues James, is not necessarily a criterion of social worth; only a Pollyanna view of the world finds support for a religion of "healthy-mindedness." The religion of the "sick soul," on the other hand, is more realistic in facing the whole of life, the good and the bad. Confrontations of this sort often result in conversions to some moral purpose, and these contribute not only to the unification of the self but also to the betterment of mankind. Mysticism is defined as that form of experience by which man comes into contact with elements in the universe beyond his comprehension through ordinary sensory or intellectual processes. James found that such experiences tend to be optimistic (the universe is revealed as ultimately good) and monistic (the universe is represented as unified), and because of their ineffability are of value only to those who experience them. It was natural that James should support psychical research in the United States, and to this end he helped organize a group in 1884 similar to the Society for Psychical Research founded in England two years earlier.

Other men gained prominence during this early period in American psychology. The Jamesian view of the biological utility of intellectual activity appealed to functionalists such as James Baldwin and G. Stanley Hall. Baldwin taught genetic psychology mostly at Princeton (writing several theoretically oriented books, one of the more interesting being *Mental Development in the Child and the Race*, 1895), and Hall, fresh from Leipzig and Wundt, established the first American psychological laboratory at Johns Hopkins University in 1883. They both played important roles in the birth of journals, reference works and professional organizations. In 1887 Hall started the first psychological journal in America, the *American Journal of Psychology;* four years later, after becoming president of Clark University, he launched the *Pedagogical Seminary* (later to be called *Journal of Genetic Psychology*) as a storehouse for research in child psychology. Finally, providing leadership in the establishment of the American Psychological Association, Hall became its first president in 1892. Baldwin's efforts (along with those of James Cattell) led to the founding of the *Psychological Review* (1894), and later the *Psychological Bulletin* (1904); he also edited a 1,500-page *Dictionary of Philosophy and Psychology* (1901–2).

Both men made contributions to psychology of another sort. Baldwin, working in the area of developmental psychology, theorized intelligently and convincingly on diverse topics, including how children perceive the world (e.g., at an early age the child does not clearly distinguish himself from his surroundings, but *projects* his own feelings of bodily movement into the movements of external objects); Hall offered, among other ideas, a recapitulation theory of human development which concentrates on the similarities between evolutionary modification and individual growth (e.g., the clinging reflex in the young human infant recapitulates the arboreal behavior of his simian ancestors). Hall's rather formidably titled book, *Adolescence: Its Psychology and Its Relations to Physiology, Anthropology, Sociology, Sex, Crime, Religion, and Education* (1904) demonstrates in no uncertain terms his global approach to human development. Adolescence was seen as a marginal period when rapid physical growth and bodily awkwardness made childhood habits impractical and adult behavior inappropriate. The individual at this stage of development, Hall affirmed, depended largely upon inherited racial habits, and observations of such phenomena might well furnish evidence of the genetic origins of human behavior.

Of particular importance, because it served to further emancipate American psychology from German influence, was Baldwin's heated debate with Titchener over the nature of reaction times. Titchener, taking data from trained introspectionists, favored a difference between sensorial and muscular reactions, which he considered to be a generalizable phenomenon of the mind; while Baldwin, citing data from unpracticed observers, argued against what he believed to be the artificialities of the structuralist's approach to psychology. Instead of two types of *reactions,* Baldwin found two types of *reactors* (sensory and motor). The controversy set in bold relief the German emphasis on establishing laws of the generalized mind versus the American concern for individual differences. It was later "solved" by J. R. Angell and A. W. Moore (1896), who showed that both Baldwin and Titchener were correct, given their respective positions. For the experienced observer the sensorial reactions were always longer (about one tenth of a second) than the muscular, because of the mental restrictions imposed by training, whereas the responses of the unpracticed subject were more influenced by idiosyncratic factors typical of those which are given play in natural situations.

C. *Functionalism at Chicago and Columbia Universities*

1. *Pragmatism.* Growth of functional psychology was dependent in large measure upon developments in the philosophy of pragmatism. Like most other philosophical systems, pragmatism can be traced to the early Greeks Socrates and Aristotle, and the British Empiricists Berkeley and Hume. Kant (1788) used the word "pragmatic" in discussing the primary importance of practical reason, i.e., "councils of prudence" as different from "rules of skill" and "commands of morality." We look to Charles Sanders Peirce (1878) and William James for more explicit formulations of pragmatism. Peirce, the brilliant American philosopher, gave the pragmatic maxim as follows: "In order to ascertain the meaning of an intellectual conception one should consider what practical consequences might conceivably result by necessity

from the truth of that conception; and the sum of these consequences will constitute the entire meaning of the conception." Accepting this basic formulation of pragmatism, James sought to extend its application to questions of morals and religion. He, but not Peirce, would accept the conception of God if it provided satisfaction for the individual. James also made pragmatism central to his approach to knowledge and thinking. To paraphrase him, *man's thinking is first and last and always for the sake of his doing.* If this be granted, then it behooves psychologists to study the mental processes of perception, emotion, volition and thought as functions of the biological organism in its adaptation to, and control of, its environment.

John Dewey's *Psychological Review* article "The Reflex Arc Concept in Psychology" (1896) is considered by some historians to be the starting point of functionalism as a definite movement in the United States. Dewey argued, as did James, against the structuralists that psychophysiological activity loses its meaning by analysis into parts or elements. Taking the reflex-arc concept as an example, he describes it as an indivisible coordination of stimuli and responses— one without the other being meaningless. Sound falling on deaf ears is not a stimulus, because it elicits no response; movement is not a response if there is no discernible stimulus causing it. In Dewey's use of the concept, the reflex becomes a mechanism for effecting a successful (i.e., adaptive or need-reducing) coordination between specific environmental and bodily events.

A student of Hall at Johns Hopkins, Dewey later went to the University of Chicago, where he advanced functionalism as a coherent point of view and influenced others to join his ranks. The American philosopher Henry Aiken divides Dewey's professional career into three periods: first as a transcendentalist and Hegelian, then joining forces with Peirce and James as a pragmatist, and finally as a logician and epistemologist. From the "middle period" on Dewey was opposed to all forms of systematic obfuscation inherent in traditional philosophy. He was, in a most important sense, a realist for whom facing reality is the only valid form of liberation. The primary lesson Dewey sought to draw, according to Aiken, is a moral one, that human affairs—societies, institutions, practices, disciplines, individual lives—are far more malleable than past philosophers could have dreamed. And it was with great faith in the efficacy of human intelligence and the methods of science that Dewey inspired American functionalism.

2. *Functionalism as a quasi system.* One of the more explicit and detailed statements of how functionalism and structuralism differed came from James Rowland Angell in a presidential address to the American Psychological Association ("The Province of Functional Psychology," published in the *Psychological Review,* 1907). Angell had been at Chicago with Dewey and came to share with the older scholar a keen interest in the functional approach to human behavior. In his address, he criticized the structuralist for not dealing with the *how* and the *why* of consciousness. This was only partly true, since Titchener, as indicated earlier in this chapter, was also interested in determining how the elements of consciousness become synthesized into mental compounds. But Angell was correct in pointing out the structuralist's disdain for purpose. Titchener had justified the structuralist's stand on this issue as early as 1898 in arguing, rather paradoxically, that functionalism (psychology of the *Is-for*) had been around for a long time with little success, while structuralism (psychology of the *Is*) was comparatively new. As Boring writes, Titchener was not against functionalism, but he thought it high time that the efforts of psychologists be directed toward the rigor and precision offered by structuralism. Angell disagreed: Why pursue the sterile even if it is new? Old concerns are not necessarily

rendered valueless by ineffective means of study. Psychologists are not remiss in studying the "utilities of consciousness" save when they do so unimaginatively.

Evidence of Angell's influence is best seen in the number of eminent psychologists who received their doctorates during his twenty-six-year tenure at Chicago. Watson, Carr, Bingham, and Hunter are a few of the fifty or so that carried on (with varying degrees of adherence) in the functionalist's tradition.

3. *Other philosophical and methodological considerations*. The fundamental point of functional psychology was made by William James. Dewey and Angell made it more explicit. The contributions of Harvey Carr (1925), Angell's successor at Chicago, were more the expositions and extension of his predecessors' views than anything new. His approach to the mind-body problem was straightforward. Mental activity, the subject matter of psychology, was conceived of as psychophysical: psychical to the extent that the individual is aware of it, and physical in that it is a reaction of the physical organism. This is not to be construed as mind-body dualism, for what Dewey had done with the stimulus-response relationship, Carr was doing for the mind-body relationship—establishing that one without the other is mere abstraction.

As to whether or not functional psychology was teleological, Carr distinguished between *proximate* and *consequent* conditions of behavior. Proximates of an act are defined as those conditions existing prior to or concurrent with the execution of the act; while consequents follow as a result of the act. Teleological explanation is avoided, stated Carr, provided that one accounts for a particular act in terms of proximate and not consequent conditions, e.g., an animal eats not because of its expectations of as satisfaction from a full stomach but due to the relation obtaining between certain internal gastrointestinal conditions and the sight, smell and taste of food. Thus, behavior is seen as resulting from the pushes of past and present conditions, and not from the pulls of future ones. It is apparent that Carr was speaking not only for the tough-minded functionalist but for the behaviorist as well.

Carr tried his hand at answering the criticism that functionalism was mere technology (since it dealt with the utility of mental activity) and not "pure" science. This may be, argued Carr somewhat paradoxically, but if pure science really be pure (i.e., combining rigorous methods with disinterest in outcome), it can support no concern whatever regarding the practical application of its discoveries. And any preference for nonutilitarian over utilitarian results (as desired by Titchener) is a violation of this spirit of pure science. Carr's contribution seems to be that *method* more than subject matter, or the use to which it is put, determines the scientific value of any enterprise.

4. *Individual differences.* Substantive work on individual differences, the one conspicuous feature of functional psychology in America, was the single greatest achievement of James Cattell. Before his impressive tenure at Columbia University, Cattell spent three productive years in Germany with Wundt at Leipzig (1883–1886) using the then conventional reaction-time experiment as a means of studying the not quite German problem of individual differences. Another year (1887) at Cambridge University and contact with Sir Francis Galton strengthened Cattell's interests in the field. Although Cattell admired Galton, he thought that psychology in America would have taken much the same path had the great Englishman not lived.

Returning to the United States, Cattell continued his psychophysical research at the University of Pennsylvania. A characteristic study of this period had to do with estimating the time it took subjects to discriminate between two disparate stimuli (hypothesizing an inverse relationship between size of the difference and discrimination time). Cattell's move to Columbia in 1891 might be considered the beginning of his career in functional or dynamic psychology. In twenty-six years as head of the experimental laboratory at Columbia he did research on an impressive array of topics, but with particular concentration on an area he chose to call *capacity psychology*—its main thrust being the study of the individual capacity to perform tasks. *Mental tests* (a term he introduced), consisting of measurements similar to those used in Galton's anthropometric laboratory (visual acuity, reaction time for sound, rate of movement, etc.), were given to large groups of college students for the first time. The more cognitively oriented intelligence tests devised in France by Binet and Simon, however, eventually won the preference of the majority of investigators.

Cattell did other applied research while at Columbia. Besides working on reaction-time and word-association experiments (starting on these while at Leipzig), he also pursued topics such as the tachistoscopic investigation of attention (discovered that the time it takes to see and name a particular object decreases as the number of simultaneously presented objects increases up to a maximum of about five), the psychophysics of perception (argued that such studies do not reveal the existence of "sense units" as suggested by Fechner, but showed only the range of error in the "organic response" of the subjects), and the measurement of scientific eminence. On this last topic, Cattell devised the *method of order of merit* (1902) whereby a list of appropriate items are ranked in serial order according to some arbitrary criterion of value. Thus, he was able to arrive at generalized opinion by averaging across individual judgments about famous scientists. The technique was actually used in compiling lists of eminent scientists appearing in the *American Men of Science*, which Cattell edited from 1906 to 1938. His other editorships (*Psychological Review; Popular Science Monthly; Science; American Naturalist; School and Society*) and professional posts (promoter and consultant of the Psychological Corporation—an organization which provided expert psychological services to industry and the public—and president of the Ninth International Congress of Psychology, 1929) attest to Cattell's prestige in the world of early twentieth-century science.

5. *Evolutionary adaptation.* Edward Thorndike, whose contributions to animal psychology are discussed in Chapter VIII of this book, went to Columbia first as a graduate student and then as a professor (1897–1940). Cattell was there; the atmosphere, to quote American psychologist Edna Heidbreder (*Seven Psychologies*, 1933), was one "of curves of distribution, of individual differences, of the measurement of intelligence and other human capacities . . . psychology [did] not lead a sheltered life . . . it [rubbed] elbows with biology, statistics, education, commerce, industry, and the world of affairs." It was only natural that Thorndike would respond positively to Cattell's suggestion that he try to apply animal techniques in the study of human behavior. Success was immediate. The classic paper on transfer of training ("The Influence of Improvement in One Mental Function upon the Efficiency of Other Functions," *Psychological Review*, 1901), by Thorndike and R. S. Woodworth, came out at the turn of the century.[5] Other equally significant papers and books in applied psychology were soon to follow. A partial list of Thorndike's books in the applied fields indicates in no uncertain terms the strength of his contributions to functional psychology: *Educational Psychology* (1903); *An Introduction to the Theory of Mental*

---

[5] Robert Sessions Woodworth (1918), another longtime member of the psychology department at Columbia, agreed with Thorndike that transfer of training results from the activity of common neural bonds in the two mental functions involved. In reacting to the imageless-thought controversy, Woodworth added to the sophistication of connectionism by stating (on the basis of his own experimentation) that certain conscious processes exist which have no discernible sensory character. He offered the hypothesis that the brain contains many neural, nonsensory pathways which react to excitation in specific sensory centers in such a way as to produce a perceptual Gestalt of individual sensations in which no single element can be recognized. Here is definite distinction between specific and general cerebral projection systems.

and Social Measurements (1904); a three-volume enlarge-
ment of *Educational Psychology* (1913–1914); *The Measurement of Intelligence* (with E. O. Bregman, M. V. Cobb, and
E. Woodyard, 1925); *Fundamentals of Learning* (1932);
Your City (pertaining to the measurement of sociological
values, 1939); and *Human Nature and the Social Order*
(1940).

Reference has been made to Thorndike's theory of learning. The original *law of effect* (responses which satisfy are
stamped in and those which annoy are stamped out) was
criticized on two counts: that the terms "satisfy" and "annoy" are subjective, and that the stamping in or out process
is retroactive. The first objection led Thorndike to define a
satisfying state of affairs as one in which the learner does
nothing to avoid, while an annoying state of affairs is one
in which he does nothing to preserve, often trying to end
it. Apropos of the backward (and automatic) nature of the
reinforcement process, Thorndike argued that it is an empirical phenomenon born of observation and experiment, and
criticism on *a priori* grounds was unwarranted.

Of particular relevance to human behavior are Thorndike's
five subordinate laws or principles of learning: (a) *multiple
response*—the individual has a repertoire of responses at his
disposal which he can vary as the situation demands; (b)
set, or *attitude*—the individual's attitudinal predispositions
affect learning; (c) *prepotency of elements*—the individual
responds selectively to certain stimuli of predominant value;
(d) *response by analogy*—the individual responds to novel
situations as he does to situations having similar elements;
(e) *associative shifting*—the individual learns to respond to
some neutral stimulus as he does to an unconditioned
stimulus. Acknowledging the importance of context, Thorndike added to these subordinate laws the organizational
principle of *belongingness,* which attributes the facilita-
tion of verbal learning to the degree of compatibility
between the stimuli to be associated and the existing

Gestalt. For example, in the sentence, "James Jones and his sister walked together rarely; both of them are children," the association of "rarely" with "both" is not nearly so strong as that between "James-Jones" or "walked-together." Belonging, Thorndike reasoned, involves a mental set which sensitizes the learner to particular aspects of the material to be learned.

Thorndike's *associationism, or connectionism,* as it is often called, carried over to his conception of intelligence. He hypothesized three types of intellectual ability (abstract, social, and mechanical) which depend upon the number of neural connections in the brain. Opposed to Binet's assumption of general mental ability, Thorndike developed his own instrument known as CAVD (including *completion* items, *arithmetic* reasoning, *vocabulary,* and ability to follow *directions*) for measuring the three relatively independent factors.

XI. More Recent Developments in Psychology: Other Systems and Theories

> *Indeed the measure of our intellectual maturity . . . is our capacity to feel less and less satisfied with our answers to better and better problems.*
>
> GORDON ALLPORT

A. Behaviorism and the Objective Point of View—

1. *Antecedents.* Pavlovian conditioning (discussed briefly in Chapter VIII) is the epitome of objectivity. Here was a procedure which permitted the scientist to study, in great detail, relationships between changes in environmental input and behavioral output. The organism, any organism, was, in effect, able to communicate its sensibilities via the presence or absence of a conditioned response. Pavlov's work on conditioning is, without question, a milestone in the behavioristic era in psychology.

The efforts of another Russian, neurophysiologist Vladimir Bekhterev (1907), also served the cause of early behaviorism. He was more engrossed in psychology proper than was Pavlov. He, more than Pavlov and his mentor I. M. Sechenov, who wrote of thinking as "reflexes of the brain" (1863), worked for the creation of a new psychology—a psychology based purely on objective techniques. Research with Wundt at Leipzig, with du Bois-Reymond at Berlin, and with Charcot at Paris had more than familiarized Bekhterev with the problems of psychology. His published works (of which there are approximately 600 titles), spread over neurology, psychiatry, developmental psychology, education, social psychology, judicial psychology, and aesthetics, were imbued with a monistic approach to psychology in which all behavior, from the simplest to the most complex, could be understood in terms of basic physiological processes such as conditioning. In a revised edition of Hilgard and Marquis' *Conditioning and Learning* (1961), Gregory Kimble, a present-day learning theorist, lists six of Bekhterev's more important contributions to psychology in the early years of behaviorism: (a) methods of conditioning leg and finger flexion, cardiac and respiratory reflexes; (b) the concept of thinking as subvocal speech; (c) the methods of using conditioning for testing sensory thresholds; (d) the interpretation of concept formation in terms of generalization; (e) a fairly clear statement of a stimulus-substitution theory of conditioning (that the neutral stimulus becomes behaviorally equivalent to the unconditioned stimulus); and (f) a denial of introspection as a fundamental psychological method. Considering all this, one wonders why Bekhterev is not more widely known among American psychologists.

Although his motor-conditioning techniques were preferred to the salivary method of Pavlov by most experimenters, Kimble suggests that the Pavlovian theory and terminology were more acceptable to the Americans because they smacked less of outmoded European psychology—for example, Pavlov's term *conditioned reflex* as against Bekhterev's counterpart *association-reflex*. Pavlov's detailed and precise results within a relatively circumscribed area of research also proved to be of greater use to the laboratory scientist than Bekhterev's more global approach to conditioning.

Knowledge of conditioning methods reached other countries partly through Pavlov's own 1906 Huxley lecture in England, "The Scientific Investigation of the Psychical Faculties or Processes in the Higher Animals" (which was summarized by Yerkes and Morgulis in a 1909 issue of *Science*), partly through the translations of Bekhterev's book *Objective Psychology* (in French and German, 1913), and partly also through the experimental conditioning of children as reported in German by a student of Pavlov, N. I. Krasnogorski (1909 and 1913). Conditioning research in the United States seemed to be less influenced by Yerkes and Morgulis' review of Pavlov's lecture than by the pioneering work of Florence Mateer (1916). W. H. Burnham at Clark University had aroused his student's interest in replicating some of Krasnogorski's conditioning experiments using children. Mateer's research was so successful that Burnham made significant use of the conditioned reflex concept in his own writings on mental hygiene.

2. *Formation of a "school."* According to the Iowa philosopher Gustav Bergmann (in a *Psychological Review* article, "The Contributions of John B. Watson," 1956), a school "is a group of men who propound a doctrine that is a mixture of three quite heterogeneous ingredients . . . first, a more or less articulate philosophical position; second, some methodological insights *about* psychology; and, third, a group of beliefs concerning matters of facts and law *within* psychology." These three points provide the frame of reference for the following discussion of Watson's contributions to American psychology.

Watson sought to establish for the science of psychology a truly rigorous and objective point of view. To do this, he thought it best to adopt a form of materialism which denied not only the existence of interacting minds but also minds themselves. With this bold stroke he meant to deprive structuralism and the mentalistic aspects of functionalism of their *raison d'être*—if there are no minds, then one cannot talk meaningfully about mental elements and/or the processes of consciousness. William James had asked the question, "Does consciousness exist?" (1904), declaring that "the stream of thinking is only a coreless name for what, when scrutinized, reveals itself to consist chiefly of the stream of my breathing together with certain intracephalic adjustments." But this was James as his own devil's advocate, pitting the tough against the tender. Most agree that his tender-minded approach to psychology won out. Watson (although himself a graduate from Chicago under the functionalist Angell) chided James and other functionalists for being too timid, halfhearted, and ineffectual in their criticisms of structuralism. He demanded more than a change of emphasis within psychology; he insisted on a break with the past in the construction of a new science of behavior.

As to the second ingredient, methodological insights about psychology, Watson proposed that psychology be restricted to a study of behavioral phenomena which could be ascertained objectively. The method of the animal psychologist— whereby the observer, like the physical scientist, stands outside his subject matter—seemed best suited to this enterprise. Although the conditioned-reflex technique proved to be invaluable in the methodological rubric of behaviorism, its importance did not occur to Watson until the publication of Mateer's research and the translation (by Watson and his seminar students at Johns Hopkins) of the French edition of Bekhterev's *Objective Psychology* in 1915. Watson soon came to realize "how easily the conditioned response could be looked upon as the unit of what we had been calling *Habit*." Knowledge of the most rigorous kind could be obtained using the techniques of conditioning, and its use best illustrates the uncompromising stand that behaviorism took in favor of objective methods of research. Take, for example, the problem of discovering how far out into the red and violet ends of the spectrum the human eye can see. One obvious way would be to ask the person to state at what wave length a particular colored light fades from sight. Deliberately avoiding the possible vicissitudes of verbal report (though Watson considered this a form of overt behavior), Watson suggested that the experimenter could determine this fact more objectively and accurately (and I might add, more tediously) by conditioning an intermediate wave length to electric shock, and then gradually increasing or decreasing the wave lengths until there is no discernible conditioned response (periodic reconditioning using the original conditioned and unconditioned stimuli may be necessary). The conditioning concept was of value elsewhere as we shall see in a discussion of Bergmann's third ingredient of Watson's school of behaviorism.

On matters of thought, Watson was a *peripheralist*, that is he conceived of thinking as implicit motor behavior (Bekhterev had a similar theory). Külpe had distinguished between peripherally and centrally aroused sensations: the former are elicited by an external stimulus in some sort of one-to-one relationship, while the latter (e.g., a memory image of an object) are exclusively cerebral affairs requiring no such stimulation from the outside. The mentalism inherent in this distinction was anathema to Watson. Images of any sort were children of the devil and suggested the interaction of minds. Thinking, then, could best be studied by observing its development as given in the overt behavior of growing children. According to the behaviorist, the child at first thinks aloud in that he says what he is doing as he does it. Because of social pressures, the child passes gradually from talking aloud to himself, to whispering to himself, and finally to talking inaudibly and invisibly to himself. What the theory requires is that inner speech must consist of little movements of some speech or speech-related organ. Watson proposed that delicate recordings be taken of laryngeal, mouth, and tongue movements during thought, to learn something about the "organs of thought." Examples of such research include Homer Reed's (1916) discovery that tongue muscles are active during some silent thinking, A. M. Thorson's (1925) failure to find any similarity in tongue movements between overt vocal responses and those occurring during equivalent thought, and Louis Max's (1937) discovery that the forearm muscles of deaf people tend to be active during difficult, but not during easy, thought.

Related to Watson's peripheral views of thought is his

glandular theory of emotion. The infant starts off with three kinds of innate emotional response: fear, rage, and love—each occurring as an unconditioned reflex to stimulation of the appropriate glands. Upon this foundation of primary drives the varied emotional life of the adult human is built. Conditioning a child to fear the sight of a rabbit (conditioned stimulus) by associating it with a frightening noise (unconditioned stimulus) is a classic in the field of avoidance learning (Watson and Rosalie Rayner, 1920). Implied here—and also in the research of H. E. Jones (1930) and Pavlov (1927) on experimental neurosis—is the bud of concern for the elimination of fears and phobias through various conditioning procedures. Of late, J. Wolpe (1952), among others, has thought of much of abnormal behavior not as a symptom of hidden diseases but as a problem of social conditioning which can be treated directly by methods derived from principles of learning (see A. Bandura's "Behavioral Psychotherapy," *Scientific American*, March, 1967).

As far as the dynamics of learning are concerned, Watson preferred what later was referred to as *contiguity theory*, i.e., associations between two stimuli and between stimulus and response result from the mere fact that they occur close together in time. Watson's preference for this view is understandable; it not only represented the most parsimonious explanation at a time when little was known about the nature of learning, but also provided a reasonable alternative to what Watson took to be the metaphysically untenable purposivism of reinforcement theory. Criticism of the reinforcement concept on this latter point (that the animal purposely behaved to reduce drives) was no longer justified in the more developed theorizing of Thorndike, Tolman and Hull.

A final aspect of the third ingredient of fact and law within psychology to be considered here is Watson's extreme environmentalism. His oft-quoted statement on this subject is "Give me a dozen healthy infants, well-formed, and my own specified world to bring them up in, and I'll guarantee to take any one at random and train him to become any type of specialist I might select—doctor, lawyer, artist, merchant-chief, and, yes, beggar-man and thief, regardless of his talents, penchants, tendencies, abilities, vocations, and the race of his ancestors." [1] In this view, the neonate is nothing more than the *structure* of its body and a few elementary innate stimulus-response connections. Only by means of experience in variegated surroundings does man become the socialized adult. The key word of this approach is obviously "structure," and since it is not clear what Watson meant—fine structure, including all the potential richness of the nervous system, or gross structure of bones and muscle—we are left to our own interpretations. Accepting the extreme plasticity of man, one can hardly avoid the question of social gospel. Watson's Utopia is much like that described in Aldous Huxley's *Brave New World* (1932), or that depicted in Burrhus Skinner's *Walden Two* (1948), the latter a totalitarian technocracy with the psychologist as ruler. And so the inevitable and highly controversial value judgment (as phrased by Bergmann): "Man is infinitely plastic and thus *can* be molded because he *ought* to be molded."

3. *Neo behaviorism and the advent of major theories of learning.* The atomistic reflexology of Bekhterev and Watson was condemned not only by the Gestalt psychologists but by men who considered themselves to be behaviorists, though of a different orientation. Edward Tolman (1932) addressed himself to the behavioral analysis of purposive acts—acts which are meaningful as goal-directed units of behavior. After taking his doctorate at Harvard in 1915 under the influence of Edwin Holt (a psychologist of the

[1] This statement is both qualified and justified by Watson in the material which immediately follows the quotation (*Behaviorism*, 1924): "I am going beyond my facts and I admit it, but so have the advocates of the contrary, and they have been doing it for many thousands of years." Skinner has maintained (in "The Philogeny and Ontogeny of Behavior," *Science*, September 9, 1966) that, as an enthusiastic specialist in the psychology of learning, Watson went beyond his data in emphasizing what could be accomplished in spite of genetic limitations.

"dynamic" school who was interested in such things as the causative relations between motor responses and the characteristics of consciousness), Tolman spent a few years at Northwestern University before moving to the University of California in Berkeley. The impressive list of Tolman's publications starts in 1917 with two experimental papers, one on the temporal relations of meaning and imagery (led to the Külpian conclusion that some meaning may precede some imagery), and the other on retroactive inhibition as affected by various conditions of learning. Later, around 1922, Tolman used the term "purposive behaviorism" in anticipation of his major book, *Purposive Behavior In Animals and Men*, 1932. It is definitely a *cognitive* theory of behavior, showing the influences of Watson's behaviorism (in rejecting introspection as a method and accepting consciousness only as surmised from overt behavior), McDougall's hormic psychology (in stressing the purposive or striving-toward-a-goal nature of behavior), Woodworth's dynamic psychology (in its functionalistic emphasis on action and its practical consequences), and both classical and Lewinian Gestalt psychology (in that it concentrates on *molar* or gross characteristics of behavior as man experiences them directly, rather than *molecular* or underlying physiochemical properties of behavior).

A glimmering of Tolman's system may be gotten from the general formula $B = f(S,A)$; translated, it states that Behavior is a function of the Situation and other Antecedent causes. The psychologist's job is to determine the functional relations holding between *independent variables* (S and A as internal and external stimuli) and *dependent variables* or behavioral outcomes. The fact that a given stimulus does not invariably lead to the same response necessitates the postulation of what Tolman called *intervening variables*—i.e., inferred processes between independent and dependent events. More specifically, it was the behaviorists' twofold task to establish exact functional relations between, on the one hand, the intervening variables of demands, appetites, motor skills, biases, etc., and antecedent conditions of food maintenance schedules, appropriateness of goal objects, types and modes of stimuli presented, etc., and, on the other hand, behavioral outcomes. Descriptive schemes of this kind became the model for other learning theories.

In the early 1930s, Tolman used the term "operational behaviorism" in depicting a science of psychology based upon the conversion of subjective phenomena to objective data by means of operational devices. The subjective is rendered objective by referring to the operations or acts of observation which made the private public. *Operationism* had been around in physics, as is evidenced by P. W. Bridgman's discussion of it in his *The Logic of Modern Physics* (1927). Concepts in science, the Harvard physicist maintained, are to be defined in terms of the operations used in observing them. We mean by length "nothing more than a set of operations . . . by which length is measured." All questions which cannot be answered by known observational tests (e.g., Is A's *sensation* the same as B's sensation when both are stimulated by the same intensity of light?) are meaningless until some such test can be devised. This, along with the thinking of the logical positivists,[2] made good sense

[2] Logical positivism grew out of the efforts of the Vienna Circle, a philosophical movement founded in 1924 by Moritz Schlick (other members included G. Bergmann, R. Carnap, H. Feigl, Ph. Frank, K. Gödel, H. Hahn, O. Neurath and F. Waismann). In general, it offered a method of linguistic analysis inimical to traditional philosophic conceptions of the nature of being and the meaning of life. Analysis of the kind proposed was limited to a modest but ostensibly more productive task: to discover the meaning of words and sentences by examining how they were employed in everyday language. It was argued by some (e.g., Carnap and the English philosopher A. J. Ayer) that the only meaningful propositions are analytic statements that could be verified by empirical procedures; the ethereal language of metaphysics and theology was thus rendered meaningless. Austrian-born Ludwig Wittgenstein (1938) helped tame such extremist views by insisting on the necessity for a wide variety of discourse—ranging from jokes to the "God-talk" of theologians—that has proved meaningful and useful to man. Philosophy gains not one wit by categorically dismissing nonempirical discourse as nonsense; rather, argued Wittgenstein, philosophers should treat

to all tough-minded behaviorists. It provided a way, though quite arduous at times, of clearing up and communalizing the language of psychology.

As to the important details of Tolman's cognitive theory of behavior, we might look at his treatment of the core phenomenon of learning. In 1932, he offered three classes of "laws" having to do with the learning capacity of animals, the kinds of material to be learned, and the manner in which the materials are presented to the learner. Tolman's predilection for novel terms and his rather confusing use of mentalistic jargon are evident in the following list of "capacity" laws: formal means-end-capacities (an organism's ability to establish relations between stimuli or *sign-gestalt-expectations*), discriminating and manipulating capacities, retentivity, means-end-capacities needed for alternative routes and detours in problem-solving experiences, and ideational capacities needed for "mental running-back-and-forth." He was equally productive of unusual nomenclature in the remaining two categories—e.g., *togetherness* (similar to Thorndike's concept of *belongingness*), *fusibility* (ease with which *signs* become attached to *significates*), and *emphasis* (a substitute for the law of effect, since Tolman's learning theory was largely of a nonreinforcement variety).

Later, in an article entitled "There Is More Than One Kind of Learning" (*Psychological Review*, 1949), Tolman distinguished six types of learning and the laws underlying each: *positive and negative cathexes* (an acquired relation between a drive, e.g., hunger, and an object, e.g., piece of candy—based on reinforcement); *positive and negative equivalence beliefs* (development of secondary reinforcers whereby an organism reacts to a subgoal or subdisturbance as it does to a primary goal or need—also based on reinforce-

---

such discourse as a "language game" and, keeping value judgments in abeyance, clarify the linguistic rules by way of rendering it intelligible to man.

ment); *field expectancies* (the sign-gestalt-expectations of his earlier system—unrelated to reinforcement); *field-cognition modes* (a disposition or readiness to acquire perceptual, memorial, or inferential field expectancies—also unrelated to reinforcement); *drive discriminations* (the learning of distinctions between, say, hunger and thirst drives—no laws suggested); and *motor patterns* (acquisition of motor patterns such as riding a bicycle, or typing—based on contiguity). In both early and late versions Tolman is decidedly "programmatic," failing to give any precise system of postulates and deduced theorems, as did the learning theorist whom we consider next.

In 1917, while still a graduate student at the University of Wisconsin, Clark Hull published one of his first scientific articles, on the formation and retention of associations among the insane. Receiving his doctorate in 1918, Hull stayed on as a teacher at Wisconsin until 1929, when he left for Yale University. His early interests at Yale involved research on suggestibility (authoring a classic series of experiments on the subject in 1933—see Footnote 3, p. 58) and speculation on the mechanical nature of conscious human behavior (proposing that much of it could be duplicated by machines and robots). One has only to glance at Hull's *Mathematico-Deductive Theory of Rote Learning* (with C. I. Hovland, R. T. Ross, M. Hall, D. T. Perkins and F. B. Fitch, 1940) or the less formidable *Principles of Behavior* (1943), to see how enamored the man was with the philosophy of science, with mathematics, and with theory construction in psychology. Although Hull wrote two other major works (*Essentials of Behavior,* 1951, and *A Behavior System,* 1952) before his death in 1952, a representative picture of his approach to psychology may be obtained from his 1943 publication. Charles Osgood's *Method and Theory In Experimental Psychology* (1953) and Ernest Hilgard's *Theories of Learning* (1948; 2nd ed., 1956) are excellent secondary sources on Hull.

The ambitious nature of Hull's program in psychology is best seen in his own words:

> It [*Principles of Behavior*] has been written on the assumption that all behavior, individual and social, moral and immoral, normal and psychopathic, is generated from the same primary laws; that the differences in the objective behavioral manifestations are due to the differing conditions under which habits are set up and function. Consequently the present work may be regarded as a general introduction to the theory of all the behavioral (social) sciences.

The plan was initiated with an impressive array of basic definitions (stimulus, response, habit, etc.), postulates, and corollaries of an unprecedented order of detail in psychology.

In general, the postulates begin with the representation of the stimulus in afferent (sensory) neural processes and end with a description of the means of measuring the organism's *reaction potential*. More specifically, Postulates 1 and 2 bear on the nature of stimulus reception and stimulus interaction within the nervous system of the organism; Postulate 3 takes account of the existence of innate behavior in the form of unconditioned responses of the Pavlovian variety; Postulate 4 concerns the nature of *reinforcement* (strengthening of only those stimulus-response connections which are immediately followed by the relief of tissue-need or *drive reduction*—a key concept in Hullian theory) and the development of *habit strength*; Postulate 5 has to do with the common conditioning phenomenon of *stimulus generalization*, or the fact that stimuli similar in kind to the one used in conditioning may arouse the same or similar responses without having undergone direct conditioning themselves; Postulates 6 and 7 involve the concept of motivation (i.e., biological drives and drive-produced stimulation); Postulates 8 and 9 have to do with the development of *reactive* and *conditioned inhibitory states* (the former is generated automatically as the result of bodily activity and dissipates with nonactivity, while the latter type of inhibition develops as a result of the association of other stimuli with the cessation of a response); Postulate 10, or the oscillation principle, is offered to help to account for the fact that organisms vary from moment to moment in their ability to perform well-established habits; Postulate 11 provides a reaction-threshold factor whereby the organism must be given a certain number of training trials before any measurable learning occurs; Postulates 12 to 15 specify ways of measuring the strength of learned responses—*viz.*, the probability, latency, durability (i.e., resistance to experimental extinction), and amplitude of responses; and finally Postulate 16 is offered to account for the outcome of two or more incompatible responses (the stronger of the two will win out). This oversimplified sketch gives the reader some inkling of the comprehensiveness, if not detail, of Hull's attempt at covering the field. If one were to fill in the seventeen-odd corollaries and numerous symbols (e.g., $S^H R$, $S^E R$, $S^I R$, $^C D$, etc.), he would no doubt be impressed by the systematic order of Hullian reinforcement theory, especially alongside the rather general features of Tolman's cognitive approach to behavior. Although Hull's postulate set was based on meager empirical evidence (mostly on the rat), it is subject to modifications as dictated by experimental findings.

A final theorist to be considered here is Edwin Guthrie. After receiving a doctorate at the University of Pennsylvania under E. A. Singer, he went to the University of Washington in Seattle. Guthrie's first major work, *General Psychology in Terms of Behavior* (coauthored with Stevenson Smith in 1921), came out only a few years after Watson's general textbook, *Psychology from the Standpoint of a Behaviorist* (1919). Though the books differ considerably in style, both made basic use of the conditioning principles of Pavlov and Bekhterev in treating all of psychology behavioristically. As to style, Smith and Guthrie were bent on giving plausible reasons for ordinary experiences—a style which

Guthrie has preserved, to the enjoyment of his readers, in his more recent publications.

From a theoretical standpoint, Guthrie presents a most parsimonious and general behavior system which attributes all learning to the contiguous relationships between stimuli and responses. Hull, it will be remembered, considered reinforcement in the form of drive reduction as the *sine qua non* of learning; Tolman thought it was necessary for only some kinds of learning; Guthrie, on the other hand, simplified things by insisting on *contiguity* as the one and only law of learning. If Guthrie's theory were to be given a form similar to that of Hull, it would consist of the following two postulates: whenever a stimulus is contiguous with a response (or movement), it becomes maximally associated with that response; and whenever a stimulus, previously associated with a given response, accompanies another response incompatible with the first, the previous association is completely eliminated. In these two simple statements we are given the means by which associations are acquired and lost.

Guthrie is ingenious in smoothing over difficulties which arise from his exceedingly presumptuous stand on seemingly complex matters. It might be interesting to look at two examples of this ingenuity. First, if an association is completely fixed in one trial, why does learning occur gradually? Guthrie accounts for the gradual improvement in learning by distinguishing between *movements* and *acts*: it is association of the former to a particular stimulus which is said to occur in one trial. Acts, consisting of many movements, take much longer to become associated to a varied stimulus situation. Secondly, since contiguity involves temporal proximity between a stimulus and response, how can the theory be used to explain such phenomena as trace conditioning (in which the response does not occur until some time after the termination of the stimulus)? Guthrie argues that the true conditioned stimulus is not the external physical energy (such as a light or a sound) but the *proprioceptive stimuli* (those occurring in the body tissues, such as muscles and tendons) which result from movements produced by the light, and these are temporarily contiguous to the appropriate response.

An interesting historical period in the development of major behavior systems was the era of the "crucial" experiment. It was believed that given two fairly explicit theoretical positions differing on some fundamental point—such as reinforcement is or is not necessary for learning—the experimentalist had it in his power to settle the issue by performing the deciding study. Considerable effort, lasting some twenty-five years from the late 1920s to the early 1950s, was expended in this elusive pursuit. One representative example might serve to show how resistant to refutation the most straightforward sounding theoretical position can be.

The *latent learning* controversy pitted the Hullians against the Tolmanians in experimentation to decide the question as to whether or not reinforcement (either in the form of primary or secondary drive reduction) is essential to learning. Tolman argued that cognitive sequences develop on the basis of sheer experience with juxtaposed stimulus situations (learning "what leads to what") in the absence of drive reduction; Hull, in opposition, insisted that drive reduction is a necessary condition for all learning. The first crucial experiment on this question was performed by H. C. Blodgett in 1929. He allowed two groups of hungry rats to explore a maze; for one group the maze was empty of food until the seventh trial (at which time food was introduced), and for the other, food was found in the goal box from the start. The former group did not appear to learn, compared to the latter, until the seventh trial when it rapidly caught up with the rats given food reward throughout all trials. This was called "latent" learning because it apparently occurred during the unreinforced trials and became manifest only when the food incentive (notice the important Tolmanian distinction between learning and performance) was present. Similar experiments were repeated with varying results, many times depending on where and by whom they were done! The Hullians concentrated their attack on weaknesses they saw in the experimental procedure—e.g., the absence of food in the end box does not necessarily mean the absence of reinforcement; maybe the behavior in question is reinforced by the rat being removed from the confinement of a small end box. Controversies of this sort subsided not as a result of any definite answers, but rather because of the redirection of psychologists away from premature theory testing and crucial experiments to *model* building and empirical probes into the largely unexplored areas of psychology.[3]

B. *Gestalt Psychology—A Culmination of Views*

What had Wertheimer written in 1912 on the nature of form that distinguished him as the leader of the new school of Gestalt psychology? The concept, or its equivalent, had been used before by a number of theorists. The philosophical position conducive to its development was around in the phenomenology of Husserl and the act psychology of Brentano. But in no preceding work had anyone gone beyond loose or piecemeal theorizing about Gestalt. Instead of modi-

[3] Related to this point is Skinner's provocative article "Are Theories of Learning Necessary?" (*Psychological Review*, 1950). He is especially opposed to theories of the hypothetico-deductive variety, because they are not only wasteful (witness the many man-hours spent on what now appear to be purely academic questions) but also downright misleading. In this last sense, theories often act as blinders, leading the investigator down wrong paths and obscuring for him the important relationships. Skinner believes that psychology is not ready for theory in its formalized sense, since many of the variables upon which such theories depend have not been determined. In its place he offers a "descriptive" behaviorism, in which exact functional relationships are established between clearly delineated situational and behavioral events. Skinner also argues for the relative importance of *operant conditioning*, in which the reward is contingent on the occurrence of a particular response, over Pavlovian conditioning in accounting for learning.

fying older theories (as did Mach and Ehrenfels), the German psychologist Max Wertheimer and his two most eminent colleagues Wolfgang Köhler and Kurt Koffka reformulated the problem and built anew an impressively broad psychological system. In the discussion which follows, the Gestaltists' criticisms of traditional systems will be considered before a more detailed treatment of their own contributions to psychology is offered.

Of main concern for the *configurationists* (a common English equivalent for Gestaltists) was the means of analysis used by the experimental psychologist. The Wundtians were severely criticized for dissecting human consciousness into meaningless or artificial units (sensations, images, and feelings) having little to do with the patterns in which they first occurred. Equally bad, thought Wertheimer, was the fact that once some perceptual or cognitive process had been analyzed it was impossible to synthesize without invoking an *ad hoc* explanation of the original pattern. Also subject to this failing was the behaviorists' assumption that intelligent behavior consists of part-activities which through trial and error become linked together. Such chance connections of reflexes, argued the configurationists, takes into account neither the occurrence of single-trial learning nor the importance of means-end relationships. Even Ehrenfels' use of form-quality is criticized, as are the writings of Meinong and other members of the Graz school (Witasek, Höfler and Benussi), because of its atomistic connotations. These older theorists proposed that the sensory elements are prior to, and consequently more stable than, the form or pattern in which they appear. Just the opposite is true, stated the configurationists.

In a more positive vein, Wertheimer insisted that all psychological processes, whether they be perceptions, cognitions, learned responses, or affectional patterns, must be conceived of as governed by internal laws, and not as results of artificial compounding of elements ("The whole determines the nature of its parts," to quote Wertheimer). Consider his treatment of the perception of apparent movement: when two horizontal slits, a few inches apart, are alternately illuminated at just the right speed, there seems to be a movement between the lines in the absence of any "real" displacement of objects in space. The *phi phenomenon,* as Wertheimer named the process, illustrates the manner in which a unique experience may be generated from the *relation* existing between two stimuli irrespective of any one element.[4] This was quite different reasoning from that of Lotze, who some fifty years earlier accounted for the visual perception of motion as the outcome of segmental stimulation (from a moving object) of points on the retina and the visual cortex. Of course, no such track of light results in the stationary eye. Wertheimer's alternative suggestion is that the experience is caused by a shift between two fields of mutual excitation in the visual cortex which is *isomorphic* (corresponding in form) to the stimulus pattern.

One of Wertheimer's more important concepts or laws is that of *Prägnanz,* or "the dynamic attribute of self-fulfillment, intrinsic in all structured totals" (to quote Gardner Murphy). Consider the results of an experiment in perception in which the subject is instructed to fixate a red circle on a gray background under normal illumination for about half a minute. He reports that he perceives a green border, an observation consistent with the laws of color contrast. Then, if a small portion is removed from the circumference, the subject reports not a green border at that point but a red patch. The Gestalt psychologist attributes this observa-

---

[4] American psychologist Harry Helson ("Psychology of *Gestalt*," *American Journal of Psychology,* 1925) called the configurationists the *echte* (real) psychological relativists. To quote him: "Their relativism harmonizes with their rejection of constant elements and of the importance of subsidiary factors to help explain what is actually observed. It means that we cannot tell from the parts alone what the whole will be; every situation is a function of a total set of conditions in which it is enmeshed. Once these have been discovered, the whole appears to be internally governed or autonomous."

tion to intrinsic forces within the form serving to make it "better" or "more natural" by eliminating its imperfections. Corroborating evidence came from studies in problem solving. Bluma Zeigarnik (1927) allowed subjects to complete some learning tasks and not others. In general, she discovered that they were able to recall the unfinished tasks more easily than the completed ones—evidence that unfinished structures do not "die down" but persist as psychic tension until some better configuration (i.e., solution of the problem) is realized.

Köhler (1924) applied Gestalt principles to the study of learning in apes. Taking advantage of his enforced stay on the Canary Islands (Tenerife) during World War I, he tested the behaviorists' supposition that animals learn in gradual trial-and-error fashion. In a typical experiment, two hollow bamboo poles were placed in the cage of a chimpanzee. A banana was then placed at a distance from the cage so that the animal could not retrieve it with either of the sticks. After many futile attempts to reach the food with one or the other of the poles, the chimpanzee sat back and in the process of playing with the poles happened to jam them together end-to-end making one long rod. Having done this, it immediately went to the bars of the cage and raked in the banana. Labeling this behavior *insight*, Köhler interpreted it as the active process of organizing internal (hunger, curiosity, etc.) and external (size of poles, distance banana is from the cage, etc.) conditions into structured wholes. The rather sudden means by which the chimpanzee comprehended the correct relationships argued against the universality of learning by trial-and-error. Results such as these also bore on the general comparative question of whether interspecies differences in behavior are quantitative or qualitative. Implied in Köhler's research (insofar as apes differ from less advanced animals) was the *discontinuity* in behavior—i.e., evolution produced not a single, evenly graded series of animal ability, but numerous branchings, some parallel, some convergent, and still others divergent in behavioral capabilities.

Attacking elementism from another position, Koffka (1925) rejected the associationistic theory which conceived of the early stages of consciousness as a chaos of separate sensations and feelings. On the contrary, young children respond to complex sensory stimuli in a manner which suggests that they perceive meaningful configurations and not a series of discrete events. Thus, education of the child should proceed through the integration of higher and higher levels of complexity, forgoing inadequate modes of thought for those which approximate more closely the richness of the real world. Wertheimer also made significant contributions to the psychology of thought in his little classic *Productive Thinking* (1945).

The Gestalt psychologists believe their concepts to be of great generality. Phenomenologically a configuration refers to any given totality described in terms of its immediate meaning to the observer; physiologically it consists of the entire chain of nervous events from the initial afferent stimulation through central processes enroute to efferent discharge; behaviorally a configurational response is to be understood within the context of the total situation confronting the organism. Furthermore, these configurational principles are not peculiar to psychology; Köhler, in particular, maintains that they also characterize biological and physical reality. The physicist, as *field theorist,* does not concern himself with additive groupings of matter or electrical charges but with properties of material systems in which each segment is influenced by every other. The biologist, likewise, is interested more in the study of whole individuals (an interdependence of organs) and species than isolated segments in attempting to ascertain the evolutionary significance of various body parts and functions.

Of particular significance with regard to field theory in psychology are the contributions of German-trained social psychologist Kurt Lewin (1936). He conceived of *life*, or *psychological space*, as a dynamic field within which there is a constant structuring of relationships between mental events such as needs, tensions, incentives, impulsions, and barriers. Lewin's early studies in mathematics and physics inclined him to think of these matters in terms of *topology* (a nonmetrical geometry of spaces which investigates the characteristics of figures remaining unchanged under continuous transformation) and *hodology* (a geometry of Lewin's own design having to do with the treatment of "vectors," or paths of directed magnitude, within psychological spaces).[5] His originality in fitting psychological issues to field theory gave rise to numerous studies in personality (e.g., Barker, Dembo and Lewin's experiment with children showing "*de*-differentiation" in life space—"regression," in Freudian terms —as a result of frustration) and social psychology (e.g., Lewin, Lippit and White's experiment on patterns of aggressive behavior in artificially created social climates). The importance of Lewin's work in the latter area resulted in his being asked to organize a Research Center in Group Dynamics in 1944 at the Massachusetts Institute of Technology. Although Lewin's untimely death three years later proved disastrous to the Institute, his influence lives on in the research of his devoted followers.

C. Some Clinical and Personality Theories after Freud—Environmental Determinants

Freud's theories, without doubt, have had greater impact on general psychology than any other single system. This was due partly to the very nature of his subject matter but,

[5] Conceptions of life space as a manifold in which positional relationships may be expressed stems from the pioneering work of B. Riemann (1923). The German mathematician contended that spaces, in which any dimensions and properties could be included so long as they are logically consistent, may be dependent upon the dynamics of intraspatial processes.

more importantly, to the creative manner in which the system was drawn together into a logical whole. Basic hypothetical constructs of unconscious motivation and psychosexual development gave rise to concepts so interrelated that alteration or rejection of one disturbed the entire theoretical structure. Such well-articulated theories are many times difficult to amend; what starts off to be an easy job of editing becomes a formidable task of erecting a new system. Attempts to "streamline" Freudian theory are numerous: Karl Abraham, Otto Fenichel, Anna Freud, E. Glover, and Ernest Jones have all labored toward this end. More disruptive forces are to be found in the criticisms and ideas of Adler and Jung. Their disagreements with Freud as to the nature of libidinal energy and the importance of sociological variables in personality development became key issues in the theories discussed next.

Erich Fromm (1941), the German-born psychiatrist, challenged the Freudian belief regarding the fixed status of the father-son relationship as formulated in the Oedipus theory. Man's nature, states Fromm, is largely a cultural product. Personalities are shaped by their society, and society, in turn, by objective historical, geographical, and economic conditions of life. The break with Freud was obvious: history is not man-made but man-making. Environmental factors rather than instinctual forces (libido) are paramount in determining man's personality. Man's tragic fate, Fromm asserts, is "to be part of nature, and yet transcend it." Other "dichotomies of existence" (phrased in the form of Kantian antinomies) are that man must live and die, be part of society yet exist as a separate entity. It is through creative expression that man realistically copes with these existential dichotomies. Related to this form of adjustment is Fromm's analysis of freedom as attained by civilized men. He distinguishes between "freedom from" and "freedom to"; that is to say, the average man in Western societies enjoys life relatively free *from* external duress but is not free *to* lead a truly creative existence. Happiness too often hinges on the social conformity of one's behavior.

Another basic difference between Freud and Fromm lies in their approach to psychotherapy. Freud eschewed value judgments as best he could in the course of therapy, while Fromm considers it imperative that the therapist take a definite stand on moral issues. Neurosis itself, argues Fromm, is symptomatic of moral failure; the neurotic must be taught that he too can create and live a productive life within the ethical guidelines of health and self-realization. Fromm is certainly more optimistic concerning man's constructive potentialities than was Freud.[6]

At about the same time, German-born Karen Horney (1939) also criticized the instinctual substratum of the Freudian system. In its place, the onetime orthodox psychoanalyst favored stressing cultural factors as the most important determinants in shaping personality. While accepting Freud's general stand on absolute causality (determinism) and unconscious motivation, Horney disputed the ubiquity of sexuality (thus challenging the libido theory), the universal validity of the Oedipus theory, and the critical nature of childhood repetitional patterns in the formation of lifelong neuroses. Horney had not actually rejected Freud's concept of sexuality but had wished to expand the pleasure principle to encompass all types of *satisfaction,* whether they be sexually derived or not. The instinctual status of libido was also rejected on grounds that it left too passive a role to environmental influences, which Horney believed to be of

[6] Fromm's optimism seems somewhat curbed as evidenced in a speech to the American Orthopsychiatric Association (April 1966) at which he said: "A man sits in front of a bad television program and does not know that he is bored; he reads of Viet Cong casualties in the newspaper and does not recall the teachings of religion; he learns of the dangers of nuclear holocaust and does not feel fear; he joins the rat race of commerce, where personal worth is measured in terms of market values, and is not aware of his anxiety. Ulcers speak louder than the mind. . . . Theologians and philosophers have been saying for a century that God is dead, but what we confront now is the possibility that man is dead, transformed into a thing, a producer, a consumer, an idolator of other things."

fundamental importance in personality development. This, of course, was a denial of the very essence of Freudian psychoanalysis—that libido is the dynamic core of personality from which are derived ego and superego functions.[7]

Besides satisfaction, the other important principle in Horney's approach is the need for *safety*—the need to feel secure and free from fear (emotional reaction to a real danger) and from anxiety (reaction to a situation perceived subjectively as dangerous). In general, Horney argued that neurosis results from situations in which the individual is made to feel basically insecure through lack of acceptance. Such experiences are particularly detrimental in early childhood (in agreement with Freud), although the development of personality depends more upon how the child is treated than on any rigidly determined sequence of stages (oral, anal, and phallic stages, according to Freud) the child supposedly passes through. Individual progress in the formation of personality, Horney contended, is highly variable, depending largely upon cultural factors. Likewise, neurosis was not conceived of as the outcome of difficulties arising in the sexual life of the individual but as a product of serious conflicts between the person and his social environment. If this be the case, society breeds neurosis in proportion to its capacity to cause chronic personal insecurity.

Deviating farther, perhaps, from Freudian beliefs than any other theorist, Harry Stack Sullivan (1947) followed Horney's example in postulating two basic motives in human behavior, *satisfaction* (a somatic activity involving tension

[7] In *Freud: The Mind of the Moralist* (1959), P. Rieff argues that Freud's libido theory is a scientifically more acceptable veneer for his real concern in dualistic ideas, or a type of dialectical thinking which stresses the interaction of two opposite powers. Take Freud's early (1892) conception of hysteria as stemming from the interplay of *antithetic ideas* as a case in point. Understanding mental conflict and the ensuing state of *ambivalence*, then, becomes the important concern of the psychoanalyst. Only at a later date was he to substitute the more naturalistic theory of libidinal energies. (Joseph Rychlak, an American psychologist at St. Louis University, who is currently writing a book on the dialectical versus the demonstrative approach to knowledge in psychology, emphasizes this point.)

and its relief) and *security* (a cultural phenomenon). Childhood experiences play a significant role in Sullivan's conception of personality growth. Particular emphasis is placed on the kinds of *interpersonal relationships* the child has with his parents and with other children and adults. Since the parents are actually the embodiment of cultural norms, the child's adjustments (or lack of same) to parental controls serves as an indicator of future adjustments in society at large. Sullivan believes that the young child is capable of *empathy* ("emotional contagion or communion"), and consequently prone to comfort or discomfort depending upon the degree of friendliness of attitude exhibited by the parents. Anxiety often results from feelings of insecurity and uneasiness in such situations, and it is regarded by Sullivan as a socially produced muscular tension. Prolonged anxiety, stemming from early childhood experiences and exacerbated by similar encounters later in life, interfere with healthy mental and physical development.

Sullivan has had much to write on the nature of personality growth and the various modes of experience and stages of development. Using his own terms, he conceptualizes human experience as moving through three different "modes": *prototaxis* (inarticulate, hazy experience in infancy); *parataxis* (differentiated, though prelogical experience that "takes on personal meaning" for the young child); and *syntaxis* (social experience in which one's views are validated against those of others). It is with this final experiential mode that Sullivan finds most to say. In sum, he believes that any valid analysis of adult personality must be directed to interpersonal situations, i.e., studying the Gestalt or "field" properties (Lewinian) of interrelationships between two or more persons (real or imaginary).

Although Gordon Allport's approach to personality has been the least affected by psychoanalytic theory of all the systems considered in this section, it is included here mainly for purposes of comparison. Throughout its nearly thirty years of evolvement, Allport's system has focused on the *complexity* and *uniqueness* of personality. Despite the importance given to the individualistic, or *idiographic,* aspect of his theory, Allport has acknowledged the need for the *nomothetic* approach which aims toward the establishment of general laws of personality growth.[8] In his early work (1937), examples of such general laws are *functional autonomy* of motives and the organization of personality in terms of *traits*. Functionally autonomous motives are "self-sustaining, contemporary systems, growing out of antecedent systems, but functionally independent of them." This conception was antithetical to all views of motivation which hypothesized continuous development from genetically determined childhood sources to environmentally fashioned adult behavior. Allport's conception of the discontinuity of motivational development was severely criticized by the classical learning theorists (particularly the Hullians) and also the psychoanalysts who favored tracing all present behavior to its genetic (instinctual) origins. Traits, the other important principle, were conceived of as "a generalized and focalized neuropsychic system (peculiar to the individual), with the capacity to render many stimuli functionally equivalent, and to initiate and guide consistent (equivalent) forms of adaptive and expressive behavior."

In keeping with his dual approach to the study of personality, Allport distinguished between *individual* and *common* traits. Although each trait is peculiar to a person, there are common evolutionary and social patterns in all cultures upon which people can be compared. The *Allport-Vernon-Lindzey Study of Values* is one attempt at measuring an individual's common traits (theoretical, economic, aesthetic,

[8] German philosophers Wilhelm Windelband (1894) and Heinrich Rickert (1899) conceived of such terms in distinguishing between natural and historical science: "nomothetic" science aims at establishing general laws, whereas "idiographic" science (history) is concerned with particulars, especially those having significance from the standpoint of *values*. This latter meaning is not apparent in Allport's distinction. Again I am indebted to Joseph Rychlak for pointing this out.

social, political and religious) against that of a standardized group having a similar background. Traits may also be characterized, writes Allport, as *cardinal* (outstanding, all-pervasive in the individual's life), *central* (foci or building blocks of personality measured by the typical rating scale) and *secondary* (minor, appearing only under careful scrutiny).

An over-all cohesiveness exists in Allport's more recent (1955) concern for the "ego" or "self." The problem now seems to be the identification and description of the essential nature of adult personality. Not wanting to reify such concepts, Allport encourages investigation into the processes of "becoming"—i.e., the style or way of life of the normal, healthy individual. This orientation is not much different from the existential concerns (man's ethical relationship to others) of some current European philosophers.

A final personality theory to be discussed is that espoused by the Harvard psychologist Henry Murray (1938). A blend of psychoanalytic, cultural, and physiological concepts, it represents the most detailed and complex system of personality yet considered. Of central importance are the hypothetical constructs of *need* and *press*. Murray defines the former as "a neural force (the physicochemical nature of which is unknown) . . . which organizes perception, apperception, intellection, conation and action in such a way as to transform in a certain direction an existing unsatisfying situation." Press (to be understood as a perceptual process), on the other hand, refers to the power that an object or person "has to affect the well-being of the subject in one way or another." Need-press relationships were studied empirically by Murray and his colleagues with various tools of the psychological clinic, such as questionnaires, interviews, hypnotic and analytic sessions, and projective techniques. The last category included the now famous Thematic Apperception Test, which was devised by Murray and C. D. Morgan for their experimental work.

Many of Freud's concepts regarding infantile sexuality and development were used by Murray in building his own system of needs; for example, needs may be manifest or latent, *viscerogenic* (hunger, thirst, sex, etc.) or *psychogenic* (affiliation, deference, seclusion, etc.), *determinant* (needs which actually regulate behavior) or *subsidiary* (substitute needs). Needs are seen as fundamental to perceptual press in that they determine the relevance of various stimuli: one's interest in food, to illustrate with a common experience, is determined by his state of hunger. Murray refers to all need-press interactions which manifest themselves in behavior (responses to the Thematic Apperception Test or some other projective technique) as *themas*.

Murray also accepts Freudian concepts bearing on the development of personality. The id, ego, and superego functions are incorporated in modified (broadening their meaning to include cultural influences) form; as are the anal, oral, and castration complexes. He has added to these such concepts as the *ego-ideal* (a fourth characteristic of mental life closely allied to superego functions and involving the person's guiding image of himself) and *urethal complex* (involving childhood pleasures of urination and related adult symbolic interests).

Appendix A: Men and Their Ideas

> *Individuals in history achieve authenticity through their actions, and historians cannot arbitrarily deprive these lives of their meaning by judgments imposed long after the event.*
>
> **PAGE SMITH**

The following thumbnail sketches of some major contributions to the history of psychology are offered merely as a convenience for quick reference. Arrangement of names is in alphabetical order. In a few cases two or more individuals having closely related interests are grouped together with the major contributor given first. Page references to this book are given in parentheses following each idea. The annotated bibliography, given at the start of this section, is a sample of what the writer believes to be the important books in the area. Because breadth of coverage is stressed in this book, many of the works cited here are secondary references. Of course, those readers who seek more detailed or broader coverage of the ideas of certain historical figures should refer to the primary sources.

ANNOTATED BIBLIOGRAPHY

BORING, EDWIN G., A *History of Experimental Psychology* (2d. ed.). New York: Appleton-Century-Crofts, 1950. Excellent historical treatment of psychologically oriented thinkers and their systems within or influenced by the experimental tradition. It is more detailed and narrower in scope than most of the other books listed here.

———, *Sensation and Perception in the History of Experimental Psychology*. New York: Appleton-Century, 1942. A first-rate, detailed history of sensation and perception from the seventeenth century to the 1920s.

BRETT, GEORGE S., *Brett's History of Psychology* (edited and abridged by R. S. Peters). New York: Macmillan, 1953. A briefer version of Brett's original three volumes (1912–1921). It is philosophically oriented, with the most complete and erudite account of ancient and medieval psychology of the books listed here.

BURTT, EDWIN ARTHUR, *The Metaphysical Foundations of Modern Physical Science* (Rev. ed.). New York: Doubleday, 1932. A scholarly account of the shift from the medieval to the modern view of man's status in the universe. The works of Copernicus, Kepler, Galileo, Descartes, Hobbes, Gilbert, Boyle and Newton are analyzed for their underlying metaphysics.

CHAPLIN, J. P., and KRAWIEC, T. S., *Systems and Theories of Psychology*. New York: Holt, Rinehart and Winston, 1960. A well-integrated treatment of the various psychological theories as they bear on the systems of associationism, structuralism, functionalism, behaviorism, Gestalt psychology, psychoanalysis, and quantitative analysis.

DENNIS, WAYNE (Ed.), *Readings in the History of Psychology*. New York: Appleton-Century-Crofts, 1948. A good collection of primary source excerpts from Aristotle to Clark Hull. The coverage is biased toward English material.

FLÜGEL, JOHN C., *A Hundred Years of Psychology, 1833–1933*. New York: Macmillan, 1933. A particularly good account of quantitative theories of intelligence and psychoanalytic theory.

FREUD, SIGMUND, *The History of the Psychoanalytic Movement*. New York: Nervous and Mental Disease Publishing Co., 1917. A translated version of Freud's own account of the origin and early development of psychoanalysis.

HEIDBREDER, EDNA, *Seven Psychologies*. New York: Appleton-Century, 1933. Interesting and readable portrayals of the major systems of psychology: structuralism, Jamesian psychology, functionalism at Chicago, behaviorism, dynamic psychology at Columbia, Gestalt psychology, and psychoanalysis.

HERRNSTEIN, RICHARD J., and BORING, EDWIN G. (Eds.), *A Source Book in the History of Psychology*. Cambridge: Harvard University Press, 1965. An excellent collection of 116 excerpts ranging from Epicurus (c. 300 B.C.) to the turn of the present century. It is arranged by topic rather than strict chronological order. Also provided is an introduction to each section and each author, helping to maintain continuity and indicating the importance of the material to follow. About a quarter of the articles appear for the first time in English translation.

HULIN, WILBUR S., *A Short History of Psychology*. New York: Henry Holt, 1934. A cursory coverage of psychology from its origin in pre-Socratic philosophy to major systems of the early twentieth century.

MÜLLER-FREIENFELS, RICHARD, *The Evolution of Modern Psychology*. New Haven: Yale University Press, 1935. In the words of the translator, American psychiatrist W. Béran Wolfe, "Müller-Freienfels has discussed the various schools of thought, evaluated their contributions, pointed out their shortcomings without rancor, and indicated how one great school of psychological thought grew organically into the next."

MURCHISON, CARL A. (Ed.), *A History of Psychology in Autobiography* (5 vols.). Worcester, Mass.: Clark University Press, 1930–1967. The first three volumes were edited by Murchison, the fourth by E. G. Boring, H. S. Langfeld, Heinz Werner, and R. M. Yerkes, and the fifth by E. G. Boring and G. Lindzey. Entertaining autobiographical histories by numerous well-known American and European psychologists of recent vintage.

MURPHY, GARDNER, *Historical Introduction to Modern Psychology* (Rev. ed.). New York: Harcourt–Brace, 1949. An extremely readable account of broad segments of the history of psychology.

RAND, BENJAMIN (Ed.), *The Classical Psychologists*. Boston: Houghton Mifflin, 1912. This book contains crucial excerpts from forty-three psychological thinkers (Anaxagoras to Wundt).

ROBACK, A. A., *History of American Psychology*. New York: Library Publishers, 1952. A thorough account of American psychology (especially before 1870) by an American psychologist who is far from enamored with tough-minded behaviorism.

RUSSELL, BERTRAND, *A History of Western Philosophy*. New York: Simon and Schuster, 1946. Russell attempts, in his own words, "to exhibit philosophy as an integrated part of social and political life: not as the isolated speculations of remarkable individuals, but as both an effect and a cause of the character of the various communities in which different systems flourished."

Divided into ancient (pre-Socratics to Aristotle), Catholic, and modern (Renaissance thinkers to logical positivism) philosophers, the book presents an amusingly idiosyncratic version of the history of ideas.

WHITE, ANDREW D., *A History of the Warfare of Science with Theology in Christendom.* New York: Braziller, 1955. An interesting treatment of the historical relation between science and theology. In the author's own words: "In all modern history, interference with science in the supposed interest of religion, no matter how conscientious such interference may have been, has resulted in the direst evils both to religion and to science . . . all untrammelled scientific investigation, no matter how dangerous to religion some of its stages may have seemed for the time to be, has invariably resulted in the highest good both of religion and of science." [Reprinted by permission of George Braziller, Inc.]

WHITE, R. W., *The Abnormal Personality* (2d ed.). New York: Ronald Press, 1956. The first chapter offers a brief historical account of theories and methods in abnormal psychology.

WOLMAN, BENJAMIN B., *Contemporary Theories and Systems in Psychology.* New York: Harper, 1960. Broad and detailed coverage of material on classical and neobehaviorism, introspectionism, Gestalt and field psychology, Freudian and neo-Freudian psychoanalysis, and scientific methodology and psychology.

ZILBOORG, GREGORY, and HENRY, G. W., *A History of Medical Psychology.* New York: Norton, 1941. A well-written, rather discursive history of psychopathology from the early Greeks to the late 1930s.

Adler, Alfred (1870–1937). Individual psychology—needs for superiority and power (64); inferiority feelings overcome by compensatory action (64).

Allport, Gordon Willard (1897–   ). Complexity and uniqueness of personality (172-173); Idiographic vs. nomothetic approach to personality theory (173); Functional autonomy (173); Trait theory (173-174); Allport-Vernon-Lindzey Study of Values (173-174); Ego psychology—"becoming" (174).

Angell, James Rowland (1869–1949). "The Province of Functional Psychology" (141); Psychology of the *Is-for*—utilities of consciousness (141).

Aristotle (384–322 B.C.). Philosophy of "becoming"—theory of causes (6); *Entelechy* (6); Laws of association in memory—contiguity, similarity, and contrast (6); Perception as "common sense" (6); Biological classification system (96); Theory of evolution (97).

Augustine of Hippo, Saint (354–430) and **Aquinas, Saint Thomas** (1225–1274). Augustine: Introspective analysis of consciousness (9); Unitary nature of consciousness (9). Aquinas: Doctrine of Twofold Truth (11).

Bacon, Francis (1561–1626). Inductive method of arriving at truth (17); Idols or false models of conduct (17).

Bain, Alexander (1818–1903). English empiricism and Mill's associationism (70-71); Genetic method (71); A variant of trial-and-error learning (71); *Mind*, first psychological journal (71).

Baldwin, James Mark (1861–1934). Developmental psychology (138); Projection (138); Types of reactors (138-139).

Bell, Sir Charles (1774–1842) and **Magendie, François** (1783–1855). Law of spinal nerve roots (39-40). Bell: Muscle sense (24 fn.); Nature of sense receptors (40 fn.); Specific nerve energies (43).

Berkeley, George Bishop (1685–1753). Idealistic empiricism—*esse* is *percipi* (24); Empirical theory of space perception (24).

Binet, Alfred (1856–1911) and **Simon, Théodore** (1873– ?). Intelligence testing (118); Intelligence as higher cognitive processes (118); Mental age (118-119).

Braid, James (1795–1861). Physiological explanation of mesmerism (56-57); Neurypnology and hypnotism (57); Psychological explanation of hypnotism (57).

Brentano, Franz (1838–1917). Neo-Scholastic approach to psychology (85-86); Mental act not content subject matter of psychology (86); Processes of ideas, feelings, and judgments (86).

Brown, Thomas (1778–1820). Mind as unity of faculties (27); Primary and secondary laws of suggestion (27-28); Adaptation of Berkeley's empirical theory of space perception (28).

Cabanis, Pierre Jean Georges (1757–1808). Brain as coordinating center for muscular reflexes (31); Levels of nervous system activity (31); Social psychology as extension of laws of individual behavior (31).

Carr, Harvey A. (1873–1954). Distinction between proximate and consequent conditions (142-143); Pure and applied psychology (143).

Cattell, James McKeen (1860–1944). Reaction-time experiments (143); Capacity psychology (144); Mental tests (144); Method of order of merit (144).

Charcot, Jean-Martin (1825–1893). Hypnosis and neurosis as morbid states of the body (58); Sexual basis of hysteria (60).

Condillac, Etienne Bonnot de (1715–1780). School of sensationism—the sentient statue (30); Simple compounding of sensations (30).

Darwin, Charles Robert (1809–1882). Struggle for existence (102-103); Biological variation (103); Natural selection (103); Evolution of emotion in animals (103-104); Pangenesis (117 fn.).

Descartes, René (1596–1650). *Cogito, ergo sum* (18); Innate ideas (19); Mind-body interactionism (19); Progenitor of developments in psychophysiology (32); Automatic reflex action (40).

Dewey, John (1859–1952). Pragmatism in psychology (140); "Reflex Arc Concept in Psychology" (140); Chicago Functionalism (140-141).

Donders, Frans Cornelis (1818–1889). Three basic reaction-time methods—simple, discrimination, and choice (68); Subtraction method for the study of time relations in higher mental processes (68-69).

Ebbinghaus, Hermann (1850–1909). Quantiative approach to memory (91); Methodological tools, including nonsense syllables, technique of constant-stimulus presentation, and derived lists (91-92); Savings method (92); Remote associations (92-93); Curve of retention (93).

Ehrenfels, Christian von (1859–1932), Mach, Ernst (1838–1916), and Meinong, Alexius (1853–1920). Precursors of Gestalt psychology (90-91). Ehrenfels: *Gestaltqualitäten* (90). Meinong: Founding and founded contents (91).

Empedocles (c. 490–430 B.C.). Emanation theory of perception 3-4); Theory of evolution (97-98).

Fechner, Gustav Theodor (1801–1887). Panpsychism (76); Adaptation of Weber's psychophysical law (76); Psychophysical methods of average error, constant stimuli, and limits (76-77); Inner and outer psychophysics (76-77 fn.); Negative sensations (77); Questionnaire study of aesthetics (77).

Flourens, Pierre Jean Marie (1794–1867) and **Rolando, Luigi** (1770–1831). Method of electrical stimulation of the brain (34). Flourens: Method of exact extirpation of the brain (34); Different levels of the brain mediate different bodily activities (34); *Action propre* and *action commune* (34-35).

Freud, Sigmund (1856–1940). Unconscious motivation (59-60); Catharsis as cure (60); Free association (61); Defense mechanisms (61-62); Dream analysis (62); Infantile sexuality (62-63); Psychosexual development (62-63); Antithetic ideas (171 fn.).

Fromm, Erich (1900–   ). Man's nature a cultural product (169); Dichotomies of existence (169); Freedom *from* vs. freedom *to* (169-170); Neurosis as moral failure (170).

Gall, Franz Joseph (1758–1828) and **Spurzheim, Johann C.** (1776–1832). Craniology or phrenology—correlation between mental and cranial traits (32-33); Divisions of the brain as faculties (33); Localization of nervous functions (33).

Galton, Sir Francis (1822–1911). Psychology of individual differences (115); Research on mental imagery (116); Eugenics (116-117); Anthropometric laboratory (117); Correlational techniques (117).

Guthrie, Edwin Ray (1886–1959). Learning as contiguous conditioning (161); One-trial learning (161); Distinction between movements and acts (161); Importance of proprioceptive cues in conditioning (161-162).

Hall, Granville Stanley (1844–1924). Journal founder (137-138); Recapituation theory of human development (138); Adolescent psychology (138).

Hartley, David (1705–1757). Physiological associationism (25); Vibrations and vibratiuncles (25-26); Psychophysical paralelism (26); Associative compounding by contiguity and repetition (26); Synchronous and successive association (26).

Helmholtz, Hermann Ludwig Ferdinand von (1821–1894). Measurement of nervous impulse (43); Specific fiber energies (44); Trichromatic theory (44); Resonance theory of hearing (44); Reaction-time studies (68); Empiricism in concept of unconscious inference (78); Physical theory of consonance (88).

Herbart, Johann Friedrich (1776–1841). Complication (67); Progenitor of scientific pedagogy (72); Psychology both metaphysical and mathematical (72); Psychic mechanics (72); Threshold of consciousness (72-73); Apperceptive mass (73).

Hobbes, Thomas (1588–1679). Materialistic empiricism (22); Matter and motion as least common denominators of man's percepts (22); Common power of state—*Leviathan* (119-120).

Horney, Karen (1885–1952). Culture and personality (170); Satisfaction and safety (170-171); Environmenal causes of neurosis (171).

Hull, Clark L. (1884–1952). Mechanical nature of human behavior (158); Postulates and correlaries of behavior (159-160); Reinforcement as drive reduction (159).

Hume, David (1711–1776). Skeptical empiricism (25); Stream of consciousness as a juxtaposition of sensations (25); Laws of association—resemblance, contiguity, and causation (25).

James, William (1842–1910). *Principles of Psychology* (134); Stream of consciousness (134-135); Psychologist's fallacy (134-135); Transitive and substantive states of consciousness (135); Theory of the self (135-136); Theory of emotion (136), *Varieties of Religious Experience* (136-137), Pragmatism (139-140).

Jung, Carl Gustav (1875–1961). The collective unconscious (63-64); Association method in studying mental processes (64); Introversion-extroversion (64); Libido as all of life's processes (64).

Kant, Immanuel (1724–1804). Empiricism-rationalism rapprochement (28); Perception as a unitary act (28); Sensations to perceptions via pure intuitions of time and space (28-29); Perceptions to conceptions via *a priori* categories (29); Events of the mind as occurring in a "flux of time" (29); Pragmatism (139).

Köhler, Wolfgang (1887–   ) and **Koffka, Kurt** (1886–1941). Köhler: Insight learning in apes (166); Configurational principles in all of science (167). Koffka: Perception of configurations and educational psychology (167).

Kraepelin, Emil (1856–1926). Predetermined nature of mental disease (52); Mental disease in terms of causes, courses, and outcomes (52); Three major types of mental disorders—primary dementia, paranoia, and manic-depressive (52); Word-association research (52-53).

Külpe, Oswald (1862–1915) and **Ach, Narziss** (1871– ?). Külpe: Rapprochement between act and content approaches to psychology (88); Imageless thought (88). Ach: Conscious attitudes (88-89), Determining tendencies (89).

La Mettrie, Julien Offray de (1709–1751). Man as machine (30); Thought muscles (30); Hedonism (30).

Lashley, Karl Spencer (1890–1959) and **Franz, Shepherd Ivory** (1874–1933). Franz: Vicarious functioning (37). Lashley: Mass action (38); Equipotentiality (38).

Lewin, Kurt (1890–1947). Life space and field theory (168); Topology-hodology (168); Social experimentation (168).

Locke, John (1632–1704). Empiricism—mind at birth a *tabula rasa* (22); Ideas of sensation and reflecion (23); Primary and secondary qualities (23); Early associationism (23-24).

Lotze, Rudolph Hermann (1817–1881). Local sign theory (73-74); Genetic theory of space perception (74); Distinction between scientific and metaphysical understanding (74).

McDougall, William (1871–1938). Test of the Lamarckian hypothesis (112); Cognitive, affective, and conative nature of instincts (121-122); Hormic psychology (122).

Mesmer, Franz Anton (1733–1815). Animal magnetism—the *baquet* (53-54); impetus to the study of hypnotism (54-58).

Mill, James (1773–1836). Static associationism (69); Mental mechanics (69); Utilitarian philosophy (69-70).

Mill, John Stuart (1806–1873). Dynamic associationism (70); Mental chemistry (70); Logic as basically inductive or empirical (70).

Morgan, Conwy Lloyd (1852–1936). Canon of parsimony (107); Trial-and-error learning (107); Incubation method (107-108); Deferred instincts (108); Developmental stages of mental activity (108).

Müller, Georg Elias (1850–1934). Theory of complexes (93-94); *Treffermethode*—psychophysical method of right associates (94); Elaboration of Fechner's psychophysical methods (94).

Müller, Johannes Peter (1801–1858). Impetus to the study of the nature of nerve impulse conduction (43); Specific nerve energies (43).

Murray, Henry Alexander (1893–). Need-press relationships (174); Thematic Apperception Test (174); Need system—viscerogenic, psychogenic, determinant, and subsidiary (175); Themas (175), Concepts of ego-ideal and urethal complex (175).

Pavlov, Ivan Petrovich (1849–1936) and **Bekhterev, Vladimir Mikhailovich** (1857–1927). Pavlov: Salivary conditioning techniques (110-111). Bekhterev: Objective psychology (148); Motor conditioning (149).

Piaget, Jean (1896–). Clinical interview as device for testing conceptual development in children (125); Developmental stages in thought (125-126); Ontogenetic development in thinking recapitulates evolution in epistemology (127).

Pinel, Philippe (1745–1826). Scientific study of insanity (50); Personality disorders as physical malady of the brain (51); Classification of mental disorders—mania, melancholia, dementia, and idiotism (51).

Plato (427–347 B.C.). Realms of Ideas and matter (5); Psyche (5); Divisions of the human soul—reason, spirit, and appetite (5 fn.). Laws of association—similarity and contiguity (6).

Reid, Thomas (1710–1796) and **Stewart, Dugald** (1753–1828). Scottish School—Doctrine of common sense (26); Divine interposition (26-27); Faculty psychology (27).

Romanes, George John (1848–1894). *Animal Intelligence* (106); Simple, complex and notional ideas (106); Recapitulation theory of animal development (106-107); Anecdotal method (106-107).

Stumpf, Carl (1848–1936). Preperceptual nature of content psychology (87); Mental content as phenomena and mental acts as psychic functions (87); Theory of consonance and tonal fusion (88).

Sullivan, Harry Stack (1892–1949). Satisfaction and security (171-172); Interpersonal relationships (172); Childhood empathy (172); Modes of human experience—prototaxis, parataxis, and syntaxis (172).

Thorndike, Edward Lee (1874–1949). Problem box (109); Laws of exercise, readiness, and effect (110); Quantitative-qualitative distinction (110); Transfer of training (145); Subordinate laws of learning—multiple response, set, prepotency of elements, response by analogy, and associative shifting (146-147); Belongingness (146-147); Theory of intelligence (147).

Titchener, Edward Bradford (1867–1927). Generalized mind (130); Mental structure (130); Sensation, image, and feeling, elements of consciousness (131); Quality, intensity, extensity, duration, clearness, and vividness—attributes of consciousness (131); Unidimensional theory of feeling (131-132); Stimulus error (132); Context theory of meaning (132).

Tolman, Edward Chace (1886–1959). Purposive behaviorism—cognitive theory of behavior (155), B = f (S,A) (155); Independent, dependent, and intervening variables (155-156); Operational behaviorism (156); Three classes of learning laws (157); Six types of learning (157-158).

Watson, John Broadus (1878–1958). Tough-minded approach to psychology (150); Importance of conditioning method in psychology (151); Thinking as implicit motor activity (152); Glandular theory of emotion (153); Extreme environmentalism (153-154).

Weber, Ernst Heinrich (1795–1878). Psychophysical law (75); Two-point limen (75); Place sense and other discoveries in sensation (75).

Wertheimer, Max (1880–1943). The psychology of form—the whole determines the nature of its parts (164-165); Phi phenomenon (165); *Prägnanz*—"dynamic attribute of self-fulfillment, intrinsic in all structured totals" (165-166).

Wundt, Wilhelm Max (1832–1920). Analysis and synthesis of consciousness (82); Trained introspection (82); Elements of sensation and feeling (82); Attributes of duration, intensity, extensity, and quality (82-83); Tridimensional theory of feeling (83); Creative synthesis (83); Reaction-time method (84); Complication experiment and prior entry (84); Racial psychology (85).

Yerkes, Robert Mearns (1876–1956). Yale Primate Laboratory (111-112); Multiple-choice method (112).

Appendix B: Recurrent Concepts in the History of Psychology

> *Past things shed light on future ones; the world was always of a kind; what is and will be was at some other time; the same things come back, but under different names and colors; not everybody recognizes them, but only he who is wise and considers them diligently.*
>
> FRANCESCO GUICCIARDINI

The recurrent theme considered in this section is that of instinct, a particularly significant issue in the history of comparative psychology which has not been discussed in detail elsewhere in the text. With this example, I hope not only to trace the development of an idea but also, more importantly, to demonstrate that many of our seemingly modern concepts have ancient roots.

The soul theories of Plato and Aristotle mark an early concern for variety in living forms. Man was conceived of as a unique species in his superior capacities for reason and thought, while animals were restricted in their commune with nature because of their less developed psychological faculties. Plants, still more poorly endowed than animals, merely had the ability to grow. A gross extension of this distinction in living forms was the early Christian characterization of animals as dominated by blind instinct and man as a rational being with both intellectual and spiritual powers divinely implanted. This view persisted in the beliefs of the Scholastics. Typical of this period was Saint Thomas Aquinas' conception of man as a supreme being fashioned in the image of God. Animals were placed on earth to serve man in his adjustments to the exigencies of terrestrial existence. It was more humane (and convenient) to think of animals without souls, since their use as food and chattel would be empathetically indefensible were they considered on a par with man.

Descartes also deduced, as it were, two realities, the mental and the physical. The former consists of powers of introspection and contemplation, and the latter of reflexive action. Man was supposedly endowed both with mental acumen and physical capabilities, whereas to animals was ascribed solely a mechanical existence. Man could reason, deliberate, and logically deduce his own presence; animals, likened to automata, responded to their immediate surroundings in a purely reflexive and involuntary manner. Descartes believed that such powers of the mind and body are not dependent upon conditioning and learning. The superior intellect which is capable of the famous aphorism *Cogito ergo sum* is God-given, and does not evolve into being through intercourse with its environment. Cartesian nativism, it should be remembered, assumed the existence of *innate ideas*— of God, self, mathematics, space and time—the truth of which are largely self-evident.

The Empiricist, on the other hand, believed that there is nothing in man's intellect or reason that has not appeared first to his senses (*Nihil est in intellectu quod non prius fuerit in sensu*). No longer was there a clear, *a priori* distinction between the rational minds of men and the irrational minds of animals. Given their extreme environmental stand on the acquisition of knowledge, the Empiricists were forced into distinguishing between forms of life in terms of the natural potential for accruing knowledge. In this way a hierarchy could then be established based upon the relative sensory and perceptual receptivity of the various living forms. One kind of animal would be superior to another, provided that its sensory equipment permitted for a greater repertory of ideas. Man would presumably head the list, since he is capable of the greatest variety of physical and mental activity. Animals with less impressionable nervous systems are restricted in their interactions with nature and consequently are more rigid and stereotyped in their behavior. The early evolutionists and animal behaviorists drew similar conclusions from greater stores of empirical data in arguing for the biological validity and importance of the instinct phenomenon.

Evolutionary theory of the Darwinian variety emphasized the

continuous nature of animal behavior.[1] Higher forms evolved from the ramifications of lower forms in their adaptation to a changing environment. Through a process of natural selection only those individuals and groups survived that had the necessary physical and mental tools to adjust to a variable life. Consonant with this belief was the underlying assumption that differences in the behavior of animals are *quantitative* not *qualitative;* or in Darwin's own words, "the mental faculties of man and the lower animals do not differ in kind, though immensely in degree." By careful examination one could find traces of animal in man and man in animal—there was hardly a development in one species that did not have its precursor in the behavior or structure of some pre-existing creature. The branchings of animal forms proceed gradually, remaining largely congruent in structure and function with its parent stock. And only through millions of years of step-by-step change do we arrive at the vast gulf in looks and behavior separating the lowest and highest forms in the animal kingdom.

This belief in the continuity of behavior is seen in the writings of others. Edward Thorndike, for example, concluded from a large number of animal experiments that the laws of learning are the same for all animals and that the conspicuous differences in the nervous systems of animals anywhere in the phyletic scale have a purely quantitative significance. This, along with Thorndike's form of environmentalism, is seen in the following quotation from his *Animal Intelligence* (1911): "If my analysis is true, the evolution of behavior is a rather simple matter. Formally the crab, fish, dog, cat, monkey, and baby have very similar intellects and characteristics. All are systems of connections subject to change by the laws of exercise and effect." Similar views have been espoused by more recent investigators; Tolman, Hull, Guthrie, Skinner and N. Miller, to name a few, all base their conclusions about the nature of learning on information gathered from research with a few selected mammals (primarily the rat,

[1] Some historians contend that Charles Darwin made an important concession to the theological powers in arguing against discontinuity between mental development of man and animal, but not between instinct and reason—man, because he has a soul, is more the master of reason than the slave of instinct (F. A. Beach. "The Descent of Instinct," *Psychological Review*, November, 1955).

the monkey, and man).[2] Needless to say, the question of instinct was inconsequential to these theorists so steeped in environmentalism.

There were other psychological theorists, however, who kept instinct a core concept in their system. Two conspicuous names in this group were William James and William McDougall. Instinct for James (1890) was a complex network of excito-motor impulses. The mother rat's perception, for example, of a newborn triggers an innate impulse to pick up and return the pup to the nesting site. Most important in James's conception was his attempt to avoid the pitfall of teleological explanation by considering the instinctive response as its own reinforcement—i.e., execution of the instinctive movement itself providing the reward, rather than a means to some future end, such as parental satisfaction. This notion of the *prepotency* of the *consummatory response* was to become paramount in the theorizing of the European ethologist. It is also of interest that James considered man to have the richest supply of instincts and consequently the most varied repertory of behavior of any animal.

McDougall's theorizing on instinct (1908) has been discussed at some length earlier in this book (p. 121); he believed that instinct is an inborn psychophysiological disposition to perceive, emote, and act for greater survival. Emphasis was placed on the *purposive*, striving nature of this behavior. Instincts could vary on both stimulus and response ends, so that a limited number of neutral stimuli might become conditioned to, say, the natural danger sign of a hawk's shadow to a chick. Likewise, the chick's response to the shadow-produced fear could be modified somewhat in accordance with the dictates of the environment. Only the emotional reaction was conceived of by McDougall as remaining fixed and impervious to change—it is the essence of the instinct chain. The whole of McDougall's social psychology was predicated on the belief that man's social behavior springs from the body of instincts with which he is equipped by heredity. This

[2] American comparative psychologist Frank Beach has written an amusing article entitled, "The Snark was a Boojum" (*American Psychologist*, February, 1950), the gist of which is that overgeneralizations about animal behavior (i.e., conclusions based on limited research with a few species) are to be avoided by broadening the basis of study.

"dynamic" approach to social behavior appealed to other investigators, and it wasn't long before the field wallowed in its own verbiage. Wilfred Trotter (*Instinct of the Herd in Peace and War,* 1908), Thorstein Veblen (*The Instinct of Workmanship,* 1916), and Robert Woodworth (*Dynamic Psychology,* 1918) are but a few of the better-known authorities who were associated with this movement.

Another important theorist at this time was Sigmund Freud (1915), who conceived of the id as a chaos of instinctive energies originating from some ill-defined source within the body and controlled by the ego and/or dominant superego, which either permit, postpone, or deny their satisfaction. Of particular significance to personality development, thought Freud, is the innate sexual energy, or libido, which becomes attached to different portions of the body—mouth, anus, and genitals—as the individual matures. It is in relation to these sexual changes that the child develops responses to the outside world. Freud drew heavily on physical analogy, describing the apparent vicissitudes of instinctual energy much as one might describe the dynamics of rivers or electrical circuits. Conceptualizations in terms of mental hydraulics, while useful at a descriptive level, often prove misleading as one probes more deeply into the matter. (R. A. Hinde, in "Energy Models of Motivation," *Symposium of the Society for Experimental Biology,* Cambridge, 1960, believes that the same criticism can be made of other motivational systems based on a concept of energy, including those of McDougall, Lorenz, and Tinbergen. There is more to be said on Lorenz and Tinbergen later in this section.)

It was Knight Dunlap (1919) who led the anti-instinct revolt in criticizing McDougall and others for forcing a purposive explanation on behavioral phenomena which could be accounted for in more objective and simple terms. Lloyd Morgan had warned of the anthropomorphic extremes of the anecdotal school some twenty-five years earlier; Dunlap sought to apply the same canon of parsimony to the extravagances of the instinct movement. Other more detailed criticism included (a) the proliferation of lists of instincts due to *ad hoc,* or after-the-fact, explanations of behavior, (b) the vague and incomplete evidence concerning the inborn characteristics of instinctive behavior, and (c) the relative lack of concern for research into the mechanisms and structures underlying such behavior. Gardner Murphy maintains that the one single critique which struck the telling blow was Luther Bernard's observation (*Introduction to Social Psychology*, 1926) that the term "instinct" was applied, ever more loosely, to almost any type of behavioral uniformity to which some sort of hereditary basis, with or without evidence, could be attributed.

The behaviorists John Watson and Z–Y. Kuo are important not only for the role they played in the instinct revolt, but also as standard-bearers of extreme environmentalism in classical learning theory. They argued that to label any behavior as instinctive removed it from the field of scientific study. As Kuo (1922) asserted, psychologists, instead of trying to find nature in animals, should determine how nature could be built into animals. He attempted this in an experimental attack on such common behaviors as rat-killing in cats and pecking in chickens. Previously, such cases were considered instinctive in the sense that they were inborn and apparently unmodifiable. In a detailed experimental analysis, Kuo found evidence which strongly suggested (at least to the behaviorists) the marked docility of such behavior. He concluded that, although cats kill rats because of the way the two animals are built, such behavior can be modified markedly by varying the social conditions under which the animals are nurtured (e.g., a kitten raised in the absence of rat-killing demonstrates a greater affinity toward rats than one that experiences rat-killing by an older cat). Consistent with this view was the theorizing and research of Tolman, Hull and Guthrie. They substituted concepts of *drive* (in the form of "tension," or "tissue-need," or "intense stimulation"), *incentive* (both "primary" and "secondary" rewards and punishments) and *reinforcement* (either as "tissue-need reduction," or simple strengthening of "stimulus-response bonds through contiguity") for instinct, which was used pejoratively by most classical learning theorists of the period. The great hope was that all behavior, from at least the rat on up the phyletic scale, could be encompassed by the same principles of learning. Differences in structure did not seem to matter much for the classical learning theorist, but they did concern others, particularly the European ethologist.

Before discussing the major role of the ethologist, it is worth noting the reactions to the extreme environmentalist's stand found in the work of such Americans as L. T. Troland (1928), P. T. Young (1936), K. S. Lashley (1938), and more recently F. D. Sheffield (1950), H. F. Harlow (1953) and T. C. Schneirla (1956). All of these scientists argued against what to them appeared to be an erroneously simple picture of animal motivation. Lashley, using W. A. Kepner's (1925) experiments on the planarian, *Microstoma,* gave us an historic analysis of what was then known about the physiology of instinctive behavior. He concluded that in this lowly flatworm "are encompassed all of the major problems of dynamic psychology." Harlow, in particular, inveighed against the learning theorist's dichotomy between primary and secondary drives. He argued that such an oversimplified view of motivation (i.e., higher-order drives being learned through the association of various neutral stimuli with either the onset or termination of primary drives such as hunger, thirst, and sex) interferes with its proper investigation. Many of the fascinating discoveries in the field (e.g., the basic motivating nature of play, exploration, and "contact comfort") would never have been made (or recognized) had such a fallacious notion persisted.

But the main opposition came from the European animal behaviorist. Trained primarily in the zoological sciences, the ethologist is far more cognizant of the importance of studying the behavior of animal species in the context of their evolutionary development. This required that animals be observed in both natural and artificial settings, since the laboratory animal often behaved quite differently from its brethren in the field. Of the early ethologists, Wallace Craig (an American), Oskar Heinroth, Konrad Lorenz (who is still quite active today), and Charles Otis Whitman (also an American) stand out as major contributors to the discipline. Craig, in a classic article entitled "Appetites and Aversions as Constituents of Instincts" (*Biological Bulletin,* 1918) considered the complex network of *appetitive* and *consummatory* chains in the "vast system of cycles and apicycles" found in the behavior of animals and men.[3] Heinroth (1910) gave light to the significant phenomenon of *imprinting*, found in many precocial species (those that are fairly well developed at birth) in their social relationships to parent animals. Whitman (1898) recognized the importance of discrete units of behavior or endogenous behavior patterns in birds and their use as taxonomic characters. Lorenz's contributions to the field of instinct, which have spanned several decades, have been especially notable.

In a recent book, *Evolution and Modification of Behavior* (1965), Lorenz outlines two ways information can be fed into the animal system: (a) interaction of the species with its environment in the process of evolution (the information being gathered in the *genome* through mutation and selection), (b) interaction of the individual animal with its environment. The genetic information, which determines structure and function, is considered to be the behavioral substratum which is relatively refractory to modification; while information accruing as the result of habituation, conditioning, and other forms of learning and adjustment is more tractable and amenable to change. Critics (mostly American behaviorists and English-speaking ethologists) have argued that Lorenz's nature-oriented account of behavior not only creates an unrealistic instinct-learning dichotomy but tends also to discount and thereby discourage the study of the development of those behavioral units which Lorenz believes are "encoded in the genes." This is the very position which Kuo fought against in the early 1920s and 30s.

Lorenz (1938) had previously portrayed the ethologist's conception of instinct by means of a simple mechanical model involving the following characteristics: an innate capacity for instinctive acts existing in the nervous system as *action-specific energy* which is elicited by the function of an *innate releasing mechanism* (Tinbergen's translation of Uexküll and Lorenz's *Das*

[3] Sir Charles Scott Sherrington, the English physiologist, used the term "final" or "consummatory" reaction with much the same meaning in his publication *The Integrative Action of the Nervous System*, 1906. He also referred to "precurrent" or "anticipatory" reaction. (Consummatory should not be confused with consumatory. The former derives from *consummare*, to consummate or achieve—not from *consumere*, to consume or make away with.)

angeborene auslösende Schema) to various external *sign stimuli* (also called *releasers*) and/or the build up of internal states of need.[4] Instinctive behavior usually occurs in biologically appropriate situations, but occasionally "breaks through" in the apparent absence of sign stimuli (called *vacuum activity*), or in response to seemingly inadequate stimuli, e.g., preening of feathers in a situation commanding aggression (called *displacement activity*). The former behavior has been attributed to the "overflow" of tension or "sparking over" of energy within the animal, and the latter to the consequences of conflicting drives. A more intense instinctive response may be elicited by exaggerated or *supernormal* sign stimuli, such as the oyster catcher, a ground-nesting bird, which pays more attention to an oversized experimental egg that is rolled from its nest than to one of its own eggs. As might be expected, the explanation of phenomena such as these has been the topic of considerable debate among ethologists (see R. A. Hinde's *Animal Behaviour*, 1966).

In a more general vein, the concepts *appetitive acts* and *consummatory acts* have been used to describe the two facets of instinctive behavior consisting of a rather flexible initial phase of exploratory activity, and a more rigid, stereotyped final stage of *fixed-action patterns*, respectively. Instincts, seen in this light, no longer could be accurately described in contradistinction to "learned" behavior, but as an integrated complex of activity being differentially susceptible to environmental influences and serving some biological function. Also of key importance to the ethologist is the idea of *instinct-training interlocking*, whereby all stereotyped sequences of complex instinctive acts (as involved in the flight of birds, nest building in pregnant rats, aggressive behavior in mammals) are bound together by the effects of stimuli which have acquired significance as a result of learning. Thus female rats that are deprived of normal early experiences

[4] In an article on the relative significance of Lorenz's contributions to ethology ("Lorenzian Ethology," *Zeitschrift für Tierpsychologie*, Vol. 20, No. 4 [1963]), Julian Huxley, the famous English biologist, considers the concept of "unit releasers" (which "act as specific key stimuli unlocking genetically determined unit behaviour-patterns") to be probably the most important single contribution of Lorenzian ethology to the science of behavior. And to this he adds, "perhaps [it is] as basic as the concept of the gene to the science of genetics."

with solid food, wood shavings, and other manipulable objects exhibit highly fragmented nest-building behavior until they have had an opportunity to fill in the gaps, so to speak, with learned responses (Irenäus Eibl-Eibesfeldt, 1961).

Other leading ethologists have added valuable information to the major points covered here. A few of the more notable examples are: Niko Tinbergen's theorizing on the hierarchy of instinct centers in the nervous system (to account for long series of well-integrated instinctive behavior) and laboratory research on the nature of releasers (see his excellent book, *The Study of Instinct,* 1951),[5] W. H. Thorpe's learned attempt to bridge the gap between American learning theory and instinct theory (*Learning and Instinct in Animals,* 1956, 1963), and R. A. Hinde's similar attempt in *Animal Behaviour: A Synthesis of Ethology and Comparative Psychology* (1966).

It is of great interest that certain aspects of *species-specific behavior* (instinctive behavior characteristic of a particular species or subsection of the species), especially the constancy of the fixed-action patterns have been used in a limited sense by the ethologist for classificatory purposes. To quote W. H. Thorpe, "Such action patterns are items of behaviour in every way as constant as anatomical structures, and are potentially just as valuable for systematic phylogenetic studies."

Of late, there is renewed interest in the study of instinct as it applies to various aspects of human behavior. R. Fletcher's *Instinct in Man in the Light of Recent Work in Comparative Psychology* (1957) and K. Lorenz's recently translated *On Aggression* (1966) are two such cases attempting to show the continuity between the instinctive behavior of animals and man. Fletcher first considers the instinct concept historically and then offers a re-evaluation of it in accord with the findings of modern phychological research as a prelude to his own instinct theory. One of Lorenz's major points is to show how natural selection has turned conflict and even aggression among animals to useful account in the formation of social bonds. Take, for example, the

[5] In this book Tinbergen defines instinct as "a hierarchically organized nervous mechanism, which is susceptible to priming, releasing and directing impulses of internal as well as external origin and which respond to these impulses by co-ordinate movements that contribute to the maintenance of the individual and the species."

"triumph ceremony" of geese and swans, in which a pair of birds
come closely together, assume a particular posture, and sound a
striking call. Such behavior most probably originated as an outcome of the conflict involved in the close approach of the two
birds, and in the course of evolution became converted into the
most important elements in the pair-bond; i.e., serving to con-
solidate the relationship giving the pair reassurance in the face
of danger. But man—and this is Lorenz's crucial and *largely
unverified assumption*—is saddled with a "biological disharmony"
(to use Theodosius Dobzhansky's term) in that he has inherited
aggressive drives from his animal ancestors without the concomitant means of effectively and safely discharging these drives
in various "sophisticated" (e.g., modern warfare) human encounters.

It might be said in conclusion that although the instinct concept has had a long history, the most fruitful probe to date has
been a complement of systematic field investigation and well-
controlled laboratory experiments. And to this end, we owe much
to the combined efforts of the ethologist and comparative psychologist.[6]

---

[6] The benefits of interdisciplinary teaching and research are intelligently
discussed by Frank Beach in "The Perpetuation and Evolution of Biological
Science" (*American Psychologist,* October, 1966). With reference to the
exchange between ethology and psychology, he believes that because of the
interaction between the "subspecies of biological science . . . ethologists
have become convinced that learning plays an important role in shaping
the behavior characteristics of various birds and mammals, and psychologists
have come to realize that interspecific differences in behavior are traceable
to associated differences in the species genotype." In sum, behavior results
from complex interactions between *endogenous* (internal) and *exogenous*
(external) factors. A revival in emphasis on the importance of endogenous
factors appears in modern *behavioral genetics*—See G. E. McClean's "The
Inheritance of Behavior" in *Psychology in the Making* by L. Postman), 1962.

Appendix C: Glossary

*Alice had not the slightest idea what Lati-
tude was, or Longitude either, but she
thought they were nice grand words to say.*

LEWIS CARROLL

This glossary is restricted to the key terms appearing in the text.

a priori categories. Kantian synthetic forms, or "pure principles of the understanding." He recognized twelve in all, grouped under four headings: *quantity, quality, relation,* and *modality.* Without these forms and the PURE INTUITIONS OF SPACE AND TIME (see definition), there could be no knowledge or experience of Nature.

act psychology. Usually refers to the psychology of Franz Brentano who considered the mental act of perceiving and thinking, rather than the content of perception and thought, to be the proper subject matter of psychology.

action propre; action commune. Terms used by Pierre Flourens to depict both the precisely localized and general functions of the brain, respectively.

action theory of consciousness. Idea of consciousness as the facility of nervous discharge from sense organs to motor response (Münsterberg).

animal electricity. An imagined property of animal tissue erroneously demonstrated by Luigi Galvani in touching a muscle-nerve preparation with two metals (in reality eliciting spasms in the excised muscle by means of static electricity from Leyden jars).

animal magnetism. Helmont's mystical concept of a magnetic fluid which radiates from all men and may be used to affect the minds and bodies of others.

anthropocentrism. Aristotelian conception of man as the central fact of the universe, to which all surrounding facts have reference.

anthropomorphism. In comparative psychology, the practice of attributing human characteristics to infrahuman animals.

antinomy. Apparent contradiction or inconsistency between two principles or laws—e.g., space and time must be limited and yet must also be infinite. The contradiction disappears if we distinguish between the psychological real (Kantian "modes" of perception) and the physical real.

apperception. As used by Wundt, the process by which the elements of experience (sensations and feelings) are selected, appropriated, and synthesized in consciousness.

apperceptive mass. The residuum of past experience upon which any novel experience is interpreted by the individual mind. Johann Herbart conceived of apperception as the process by which a novel experience is combined with and modified by the residuum of past experiences to form a new conscious whole.

associationism. In its simplest form, a theory of the structure and organization of the mind asserting that (a) every mental event is resolvable into simple, discrete components, and (b) all mental life is explicable by the combination and recombination of these simple ideas in conformity with specific laws—contiguity, similarity, contrast, etc.

atavism. Reversion to a primitive form or type. The Italian anthropologist, Cesare Lombroso, characterized the habitual criminal as a throwback of this kind.

behaviorism. In its orthodox version (John Watson), a school of psychology which abandoned the concepts of mind and consciousness, and restricted study to the observable and quantifiable aspects of animal and human behavior. Although neobehaviorism has taken many forms, the common denominator is the emphasis placed on establishing functional relationships between independent (i.e., external and internal stimuli) and dependent or behavioral variables.

catharsis. In its Aristotelian sense, the purging of the emotions of pity and fear by means of the tragic drama. In psychiatric terminology, alleviation of fears and guilts by bringing them to consciousness and allowing them expression.

classical conditioning. As used by Ivan Pavlov, the transfer of an unconditioned response from an unconditioned stimulus to a conditioned stimulus as a result of the repeated pairing of the two stimuli in a specific temporal order (usually the conditioned stimulus presented a fraction of a second before the unconditioned stimulus) and under controlled experimental conditions.

Cogito ergo sum. "I think, therefore I am," the statement embodying René Descartes's attempt to establish the existence of the self in any act of thinking, including the act of doubting.

complication experiment. A technique for the experimental investigation of the personal equation, consisting of an observer noting the exact location of a swinging pointer on a scale when he heard a bell or click. Wilhelm Wundt used such a device ("complication clock") for this purpose.

connectionism. A term Edward Thorndike used to depict his brand of associationism, i.e., learning conceived of as the establishment of stimulus response bonds or connections.

conscious attitudes (Bewusstseinslagen). The obscure, unanalyzable, undescribable "feeling" content of the mind, e.g., feelings of doubt and of certainty, of affirmation and of dissent (Karl Marbe and J. Orth). In essence, this was a recognition of an imageless ingredient of the mind (Würzburg school) not subsumed in the Wundtian elements of sensation and feeling.

context theory of meaning. According to Edward Titchener, "meaning" is best understood as the sensory context in which a mental structure happens to appear. The meaning of a particular perception or idea depends upon the other sensations or images that happen to become associated with it, either consciously or unconsciously.

contiguity. The occurrence together in time or space of two or more stimuli, responses, or stimuli *and* responses. The cornerstone of associationism.

cosmology. A branch of philosophy having to do with the origin and nature of the universe. Many of the cosmological theories were discussed by the pre-Socratic philosophers and expanded on by Plato (in *Timaeus*) and systematized by Aristotle (in *Physics*).

creative synthesis. The dynamic mental process whereby various elements of perception and cognition become unity. John Stuart Mill wrote that complex ideas do not *consist of* but *result* *from,* or are *generated by,* simple ideas (i.e., "mental chemistry"). Some fifty years later, Wilhelm Wundt wrote more explicitly about *creative synthesis,* emphasizing that a combination of elements gives rise to *psychic resultants* that have properties which were not properties of the elements.

deduction. Reasoning from a general principle to a specific logical conclusion.

determining tendencies. The numerous unconscious predispositions which operate to control and direct the course of thought and decision (Narziss Ach). Henry Watt proposed a similar construct emphasizing the influence on judgment and thought of the task, problem, or "set" (*Aufgabe*) given the subject.

Dewey's reflex-arc concept. Conceiving of the stimulus and response as "correlative and contemporaneous" phenomena. John Dewey argued against elementism in psychology in emphasizing the coordinative aspect of reflexive behavior; the reflex is not to be thought of as a stimulus followed by a response (i.e., two discrete events) but as an indivisible coordination that is adaptive or purposeful in goal-directed behavior.

doctrine of common sense. The stand that all men have an immediate and compelling conviction in the reality of the external world and of their own minds. Thomas Reid of the Scottish School championed this view.

doctrine of twofold truth. A pronouncement by Saint Thomas Aquinas that there are two varieties of truth: religious truth based on ecclesiastical authority, and scientific truth founded on the direct observation of nature.

double-aspect theory. Positing two distinct entities of mind and body that are dependent upon a third fundamental reality of an unclear nature for their integrated relationship.

double-language theory. The processes of the mind and body are assumed to be the same, but each is referred to by different terms.

Ebbinghaus' retention curve. The generalization based on Hermann Ebbinghaus' classic work that forgetting is most rapid immediately after learning and then proceeds at a slower and slower rate with passing time.

emanation theory. Conceiving of sensation and perception as the result of material particles (e.g., *eidola*) which emanate from the object (or object source) and impinge on the individual's receptors.

✓ **empiricism.** The theory that the sole source of knowledge is sensory experience. The radical empiricists insisted that all ideas are reducible to sensations.

entelechy. In the Aristotelian sense, (a) the mode of being of a thing whose essence is completely realized, (b) the form or essence of things.

epiphenomenalism. A mind-body theory in which the mind is assumed to be a by-product of nervous processes, although belonging to a different basic reality.

eponymy. Naming great events after great innovators, e.g., Newtonian physics, Darwinian evolution, Freudian psychology. Edwin Boring is critical of this practice in discussing the importance of cultural influences (see ZEITGEIST) in the development of scientific thought.

equipotentiality. The principle that a given part of the cortex can substitute for the functions of other parts which have been destroyed. A given brain region is said to be *equipotential* with respect to a certain function if the losses due to removal of equal amounts of the region are equivalent and independent of the locus of injury. In a sense, this is Lashley's modern substitute for Flourens' ACTION COMMUNE and Franz's VICARIOUS FUNCTIONING.

esse is percipi. "To be is to be perceived"—the cornerstone of George Berkeley's epistemology.

ethology. The study of animal behavior. The ethologist is usually trained in zoology and believes that the behavior of animals cannot be properly studied without knowledge of the environment to which the species has become adapted in evolution.

eugenics. The study dealing with the improvement of races, breeds, and strains of animals, particularly humans, by means of the control and manipulation (through selective breeding) of hereditary factors. This was of paramount importance in the work of Sir Francis Galton.

faculty. Power or ability to perform any action, intellectual or physical. St. Thomas Aquinas included, (a) the sensory faculties (external, internal, and appetites), (b) vegetative faculties (nutrition, growth, and procreation), (c) locomotive faculty, (d) rational faculties (intellect and rational will). Also a main concept of the Scottish School.

founding and founded content. Terms used by Alexius Meinong in place of Ehrenfels' *Fundamente* and *Gestaltqualität*. Being fundamentally an act psychologist, Meinong used the terms in discussing the development of mental activities such as perception and conception—the founding contents are the *inferiora* and the founded contents the *superiora* in the hierarchical order of mental life. Much like Aristotle's conception of the relationship between form and matter, the *superiora* of lower mental complexions could become the *inferiora* of higher complexions in the founding of a still higher *superius*.

free association. A psychoanalytic technique, first used in a systematic way by Sigmund Freud, of allowing the patient to talk freely about anything, entertaining whatever idea, memory, or emotion that can be verbalized. In this way the patient helps uncover clues to the nature of his repressed thoughts and wishes.

functionalism. An approach to psychology in which mental processes, such as perception, emotion, volition, and thought, are understood in relation to the organism's attempt to adapt to, and gain control of, its environment—a view fundamental to the beliefs of William James and John Dewey.

✓ **Gestalt.** A German word given numerous English equivalents—e.g., *shape, form, organization, pattern, configuration*. The last seems to come closest to what is implied in Gestalt psychology.

Gestaltqualität. A term coined by Christian von Ehrenfels meaning "form-quality" or, more specifically "the quality conferred by a pattern" (from Gardner Murphy).

hedonism. The doctrine that pleasure is the principal good and should be the aim of behavior. As a psychological doctrine, motivation is explained exclusively in terms of desire for pleasure and avoidance of pain.

hormic psychology. William McDougall's brand of psychology, which asserts that active striving toward a goal is a fundamental characteristic of animal and human behavior.

hylozoism. The ancient doctrine that all life is a property of physical matter. Derived from this premise are the following conclusions: Matter and life are inseparable; life is derived from matter, and matter has spiritual properties. This idea was prevalent among the early Greek cosmologists, especially of the Milesian school (c. 6th century B.C.).

idealistic monism. A mind-body solution concluding that all of the so-called physical and physiological processes are in fact of the same kind as the processes of the mind.

idiographic laws. Objective statements having to do with particulars, especially those involving questions of values. History is an idiographic science (Windelband, 1894). G. Allport used this term to refer to the psychology of the individual.

imageless thought. The fact that cognitions are not necessarily embodied in sensuous imagery. This was a bone of contention between the structuralists (mainly E. B. Titchener who denied their existence) and followers of the Würzburg school (led by Oswald Külpe who affirmed their existence).

immediate and mediate experience. According to Wilhelm Wundt, experience understood or perceived directly or intuitively (i.e., immediate) was the raw material for study in the science of psychology, while experience obtained indirectly from instrumental records (i.e., mediate) was the proper subject matter for other sciences.

induction. Reasoning from particular facts or individual cases to general conclusions.

inner and outer psychophysics. For Gustav Fechner, the former is the relation between mind and the excitation most immediate to it, and the latter is the relation between mind and the actual stimulus. Fechner was fundamentally concerned with establishing quantitative functions for inner psychophysics.

✓ **insight.** The process whereby a solution, meaning, or understanding of a problem occurs rather suddenly, and smoothly. The Gestalt psychologists thought of insight as an *emergent* (i.e., growing out of the animal's intrinsic understanding of a situation) principle of behavior.

intentional inexistence. In distinguishing between the psychic and the physical, Franz Brentano used this term to depict "the discriminatory peculiarity of all psychic phenomena . . . their relation to something as an object," i.e., there is an object which inexists intentionally within every psychic act. This was a central concept in act psychology.

isomorphism. As a term in Gestalt psychology, it refers to the structural similarity between excitatory fields in the brain and the perceptual content of consciousness. The correspondence is topological and not topographical.

James-Lange theory of emotion. The assertion that affective states are the conscious manifestations of sensory impressions from skeletal muscles, viscera and other organs of the body. The theory was independently expounded by Carl Lange and William James (". . . we feel sorry because we cry, angry because we strike, afraid because we tremble and not cry, strike, or tremble because we are sorry, angry, or fearful . . .").

law of effect. Edward L. Thorndike's assumption that of several responses made to the same situation, those which are accompanied or closely followed by satisfaction to the animal will, other things being equal, be more firmly connected with the situation, so that, when it recurs, they will be more likely to recur; those which are accompanied or closely followed by discomfort to the animal will, other things being equal, have their connections with that situation weakened, so that, when it recurs, they will be less likely to occur. The greater the satisfaction or discomfort, the greater the strengthening or weakening of the bond (from *Animal Intelligence,* 1911). Thorndike later, after more experimentation, abandoned the second half of the law; the revision is sometimes called the "truncated law of effect."

law of exercise. Edward L. Thorndike's assumption that any response to a situation will, other things being equal, be more strongly connected with the situation in proportion to the number of times it has been connected with that situation and to the average vigor and duration of the connections (from *Animal Intelligence,* 1911). Experimental evidence caused Thorndike to abandon this law.

law of readiness. Edward L. Thorndike's assumption that for a conduction unit ready to conduct to do so is satisfying and for it not to do so is annoying; and for a conduction unit unready to conduct to be forced to do so would be annoying (from

Educational Psychology, Vol. 1. *The Original Nature of Man,* 1913); J. P. Chaplin and T. S. Krawiec (*Systems and Theories of Psychology,* 1960) point out that this law "makes sense only if interpreted that a preparatory set is an important condition influencing learning." An organism's set for engaging in or not engaging in a certain activity determines the affective tone of the behavior.

Lloyd Morgan's canon. In an attempt to guard against anthropomorphic reasoning in the study of animal behavior, Lloyd Morgan formulated a "law of parsimony" stating, "In no case may we interpret an action as the outcome of the exercise of a higher psychical faculty, if it can be interpreted as the outcome of the exercise of one which stands lower in the psychological scale."

local-sign theory. A quasi-empirical conception by Hermann Lotze which states, among other things, that space perception is "learned" through the associations of actual movement in space with the movement-produced stimulation of local sensory spots —in short, space perception depends upon sensory cues (i.e., *local signs*) which in and of themselves are nonspatial.

logical positivism. An approach to philosophy involving the unification of the sciences, especially by an analysis of the language of science and the consequent development of a vocabulary (probably physical in nature) applicable to all sciences. Auguste Comte originated a system of philosophy based solely on the positive data of sense experience.

mass action. A physiological principle that the ability both to learn and to retain what has been learned is proportional to the *amount,* regardless of location, of cortical tissue present, and hence that the entire region has some general facilitative function.

materialistic monism. A mind-body solution concluding that the processes of the mind are in fact physiological processes.

mental chemistry. The analogy used by John Stuart Mill in explaining mental states as the products of the combination and fusion of psychic elements, i.e., analogous to chemical synthesis.

mental mechanics. The process whereby the mind becomes a mosaic of crystallized sensations held together by the sole means of their contiguous occurrence. James Mill thus portrayed the process of association as one of mechanical passivity.

method of average error or **adjustment.** The subject is required to adjust a variable stimulus to match a standard stimulus. Discrepancies are then averaged over a number of trials to determine the "average error."

method of constant stimuli or **right-and-wrong cases.** For measuring absolute thresholds: the subject is asked to report the presence or absence of a single stimulus given on successive trials at varying magnitudes. For measuring difference thresholds: the subject is asked to report which of two stimuli, one of constant and one of variable magnitude, is greater; the magnitude of the variable stimulus is reduced or increased on successive trials.

method of limits. For measuring absolute thresholds: a stimulus is varied along a given dimension until the subject reports its presence in at least fifty per cent of the trials. For measuring difference thresholds: the subject is presented with a series of pairs of identical stimuli, one being varied until a *just-noticeable difference* is reported in at least fifty per cent of the trials for any given pair of stimuli.

mind-body problem. The age-old philosophical question of the relationship obtaining between the individual mind and its body. Proposed "solutions" have had to resolve the dilemma of how a corporeal substance could affect an incorporeal existence.

naturalism. The theory that the natural world is the whole of reality and that there is no supernatural or spiritual creation, value, control, or significance, that the world is wholly deterministic and, therefore, scientific laws can explain all phenomena.

negative sensations. Subliminal values derived from plotting the correlation between an arithmetic (sensation) and a geometric (stimulus) series in psychophysics. Gustav Fechner believed that the representation of unconscious psychical values by negative magnitude is a fundamental point for psychophysics.

nihilism. The doctrine that there is no basis for knowledge or truth (epistemological nihilism). Gorgias the Sophist argued that (a) nothing exists; (b) even if something did exist it could not be comprehended; (c) even if it were known, this knowledge could not be communicated.

nomothetic laws. Objective statements of a general nature characteristic of the natural sciences (Windelband). G. Allport used this term in referring to the establishment of general laws of personality growth.

Ockham or **Occam's razor.** A variation on the "law of parsimony" which exhorts against assuming the existence of more, or more complex, entities than the least and simplest required to explain the facts. Named after the English Franciscan theologian William of Ockham, who died in 1349.

operationism. The doctrine that the meaning of a concept is given by a set of operations. More explicitly, "In general, we mean by any concept nothing more than a set of operations; the concept is synonymous with the corresponding set of operations." (P. W. Bridgman, *The Logic of Modern Physics*, 1927.)

panpsychism. A form of metaphysical idealism which attributes psychic qualities to the whole of nature. The *monadology* of Gottfried Leibnitz, in which monads are conceived of as the real atoms of nature, is a classic example of panpsychism.

personal equations. Systematic errors in astronomical observation originating in the observer and not from instrumental or atmospheric conditions. The *absolute* personal equation refers to the degree of difference between the observer and the "true" time, while differences between individual observers are known as *relative* personal equations.

phenomenology. A term usually attributed to Edmund Husserl, who defined it as the descriptive analysis of subjective processes (*Erlebnisse*). Actually the term had been around before with many different connotations, but Husserl was the first to apply the name *Phänomenologie* to an entire philosophy.

phi phenomenon. An illusion of apparent movement resulting when two nearby lights are flashed in rapid alternation. Max Wertheimer used this phenomenon as an illustration of certain basic Gestalt principles.

phrenology. Johann Spurzheim's term for the system of belief that conformations of the skull are an index of personality traits. Referred to earlier by Franz Gall as *craniology*.

pneuma. The breath of life. Aristotle, the Stoics, and the Epicureans used the concept to denote spirit, vital force, or psychic energy.

pragmatism. The philosophy which holds that concepts can best be validated on the basis of their practical results. Its inception is attributed to Charles Peirce and somewhat later to William James ("that the end of man is action"), but also implied in the views of earlier philosophers, including Socrates, Aristotle, Berkeley, and Hume.

prägnanz. A Gestalt principle which holds that percepts and cognitions take the best form possible under the circumstances —e.g., an unclosed circle appears closed when seen rapidly.

primary and secondary qualities. The inherent characteristics of bodies—such as solidity, extension, figure, motion, rest and number—are primary whereas more variable and subjective qualities—such as tastes, smells, sounds and colors—are secondary.

primitive animism. The belief that natural phenomena, including rocks, plants, waves, the wind, etc., are alive and have souls.

prior-entry phenomenon. Researchers on the personal equation discovered that in the simultaneous presentation of two stimuli one will be perceived before the other if it has been anticipated and attention has been drawn to it.

psyche. For Aristotle, the vital principle; the formal cause, essence, or entelechy of a natural organic body. In more modern use, it is the mind, conceived of as reaching all regions of the body and serving to coordinate the total organism to the demands of the environment.

psychic mechanics. An early quasi-mathematical attempt by Johann Herbart to account for the dynamic properties of the mind. Herbart argued that ideas are active and strive to become conscious. If they are compatible with ideas already existing in consciousness, they combine harmoniously into new wholes; but if they conflict with the prevailing ideas, the stronger ones win out.

psychologist's fallacy. Assumption that when one reduces a mental complex to its supposed elements (in the manner of structuralists), the parts must have been there all along and are the essence of the complex. This was William James's criticism of the Titchenerian practice of breaking up consciousness into its imagined parts.

psychophysical interactionism. A dualistic theory of the mind-body relationship, usually attributed to René Descartes, which asserts a bidirectional causal influence (via the pineal gland for Descartes) between mental and physical activities.

psychophysical parallelism. A mind-body solution involving the existence of two distinct realities which do not interact but function in parallel fashion much as do two clocks running at the same speed and showing the same time.

pure intuitions of space and time. In the *Critique of Pure Reason*, Immanuel Kant attempts a thorough inventory of all synthetic, *a priori*, transcendental forms existent in the knowledge of Nature. Two such forms or "intuitions" (*Anschauungen*) of sensibility are those of space and time; hence, knowledge of the world, irrespective of its sensory content, is always of necessity something in space and time. Intuitions of this kind, argued Kant, are both "empirically real" (due to their presence in everyday experience) and "transcendentally ideal" (because the mind "imposes" them on sense data).

rationalism. A method or theory of philosophy in which the criterion of truth is intellectual and deductive, and not sensory and inductive.

realism. A theory in which universals (e.g., the ideas of man, tree, etc.) are equated with, or sometimes considered superior to, actual physical particulars.

reify. To treat a mental abstraction as a concrete material object—e.g., G. E. Stahl's seventeenth-century suggestion that "phlogiston" was the actual matter of fire. Concept is attributed to Polish logician Tadeusz Kotarbiński.

solipsism. The theory that the self can be aware of nothing but its own experiences and mental states; hence, the external world including other persons is a representation of the self and has no independent existence.

specific fiber energies. A logical extension of the theory of specific nerve energies stating that individual nerves themselves include fibers which give rise to different qualities of sensation—

e.g., the optic nerve has fibers sensitive to red, yellow and blue light. (The concept is usually attributed to Helmholtz.)

specific nerve energies. A theory, usually attributed to Johannes Müller, stating that sensation consists of an awareness of the properties of the sensory nerves themselves, and that each sensory nerve has its own characteristic energy or quality.

stream of consciousness. A metaphor used by William James in characterizing thought as a process of continuous change and interdependence. James entitled a chapter in his *Principles of Psychology* "The Stream of Thought."

stimulus error. The process of confounding the learned meanings of the objects being considered introspectively with the sensory content itself. The term was coined by Edward Bradford Titchener.

structuralism. A major school of psychology of the late nineteenth and early twentieth centuries depicting the science of psychology as the study of consciousness through the careful analysis of introspective reports. Edward Titchener is most closely allied with this movement which, in essence, is a rigorous simplification of Wundtian psychology.

tabula rasa. Literally, a blank tablet. The empiricists likened the mind to a blank slate upon which experience records impressions.

teleology. In general, the theory of purpose, ends, goals, final causes, values, etc. As conceived of by the vitalist, it is the belief that natural phenomena are determined not only by mechanical causes but by an all-pervasive design or purpose in nature.

theriomorphism. Attributing infrahuman animal characteristics to man.

trained introspection. The method used by the structuralists, especially by Edward Titchener and his followers. It involves the systematic observation by the experiencing subject of his own experiences, with particular care taken to avoid confusing learned meanings with psychological processes of perception (i.e., the stimulus error).

trial-and-error learning. Edward Thorndike defined this term as the kind of learning which proceeds in a somewhat random manner and without explicit recognition of the connection between the behavior and the resolution of the problem situation. Movements which lead to reward are more frequently repeated in subsequent trials, and those which fail gradually disappear. Alexander Bain made use of various views of Herbert Spencer in anticipating the importance of "random" movements in the learning of correct responses.

tridimensional theory of feeling. Wilhelm Wundt theorized that feelings could vary along three dimensions: (a) pleasantness-unpleasantness, (b) strain-relaxation, (c) excitement-depression. According to this theory, any given feeling might at the same instant be pleasant, tense, and depressed.

unconscious inference (unbewusster Schluss). The empiricist doctrine of Hermann Helmholtz which emphasizes the importance of past experience in the seemingly automatic nature of present perception; that is, perception of, say, space, is not an inherent condition of the mind, but an inferred quality brought rapidly to present perception from the observer's past experience with objects and movements in space.

vibratiuncles. A term coined by David Hartley to refer to the hypothetical condition of the body and mind following motor and sensory stimulation. These diminutive physiological vibrations were assumed to parallel ideas.

vicarious functioning. The substitution of neighboring neural cells for specific cortical loss through injury. One brain region functions vicariously for another if the habits lost following removal of the latter can be relearned providing the former is intact (attributed to the research of Franz).

Weber-Fechner law. A principle of psychophysics which expresses quantitatively the relation between the intensity of a stimulus and the intensity of the resultant sensation. Ernst Weber stated that for each noticeable difference in sensation the stimulus must vary by a constant fraction. Gustav Fechner revised "Weber's Law" into the formula $S = K \log R$; i.e., sensation varies arithmetically with the logarithm of the stimulus. This implied that each noticeable difference in sensation be regarded as a "sense unit," equivalent in value to every other just-noticeable difference.

Zeitgeist. Literally, the spirit of the age; more specifically, the trend of thought and feeling of a period. This is a major concept in Edwin Boring's view of the history of psychology—"The truth seems to be that thinking goes on within the culture, that the cultural forces are tremendously complex, that multiple causation is the rule, that a given decision often is a necessary, even if insufficient, cause of an historical event, but that the man who made the decision may not have been necessary. Someone else could have made the decision, perhaps under these conditions would have made it, thus becoming the means by which the *Zeitgeist* prevails." (*A History of Experimental Psychology*, Appleton-Century-Crofts, 1950). In "Psychology: A Prescriptive Science" (*American Psychologist*, June, 1967), R. I. Watson points out that the *Zeitgeist* theory does not "account for differential reaction to the same climate of opinion. Plato and Aristotle, Hobbes and Spinoza, Hume and Rousseau, each experienced the same *Zeitgeist* but also had idiosyncratics . . . allegiances."

Name Index

Abélard, P., 10
Abraham, K., 65, 169
Ach, N., 88, 89, 132, 201
Actuarius, J., 49
Adler, A., 64, 120, 169
Adler, H. M., 47Q
Agar, W. E., 112n
Agrippa, C., 49-50
Aiken, H., 140-141
Allport, F., 121
Allport, G. W., 148Q, 172-174, 204, 208
Anaxagoras, 95
Anaximander, 3, 95, 98n
Anaximenes, 3, 95
Angell, F., 129
Angell, J. R., 139, 141-142, 151
Anselm, St., 9-10
Aquinas, T. St., 10-11, 99, 187, 201, 203
Arago, D. F., 67
Ardrey, R., 15, 95Q
Aretaeus, 48
Aristarchus, 13n
Aristophanes, 5n
Aristotle, 6, 7, 8, 10, 60n, 85, 90, 96-97, 98, 99, 139, 187, 198, 199, 200, 202, 203, 209, 213
Asclepiades, B., 48
Astruc, J., 40-41
Augustine, St., 5n, 9, 21n, 90, 99
Aurelianus, C., 48-49
Averroës, 10n
Avicenna, 49
Ayer, A. J., 156n

Bacon, F., 17, 99
Bain, A., 70-71, 72n, 107, 212
Baldwin, J. M., 137-139
Bandura, A., 153
Bard, P., 136n
Barker, R. G., 168

Barnett, S. A., 107n
Bayle, A. L. J., 53
Beach, F. A., 189n, 190n, 197n
Beer, T., 108-109
Bekhterev, V. M., 148-149, 151, 152, 154, 160
Bell, C., 24n, 32, 39-40, 43
Bell, S., 62n
Bentham J., 69, 70, 120
Benussi, V., 164
Berenger, 10
Bergmann, G., 150, 152, 154, 156n
Berkeley, G., 10n, 19n, 20, 24, 26, 27, 28, 29, 71, 78, 139, 202, 209
Bernard, C., 45
Bernard, L., 122-123, 192
Bernheim, H., 57-58, 60-61
Bernstein, J., 43
Bessel, F., 66-67, 115
Bethe, A., 108-109
Binet, A., 118-119, 144, 147
Bingham, W. V., 142
Blodgett, H. C., 162
Blyth, E., 102n
Boethius, A. M. S., 18n
Boll, F., 84n
Bon, Le, G., 121
Bonnet, C., 30-31, 100
Boring, E. G., 36, 57, 59, 70, 72n, 76, 91, 93, 133, 141, 176r, 178r, 202, 213
Bouillaud, J., 35
Bowen, C. D., 17n
Brahe, T., 13, 14, 16n
Braid, J., 56-57
Bregman, E. O., 146
Brentano, F., 85-87, 90, 198, 204
Brett, G. S., 177
Breuer, J., 59-61
Bridgeman, P. W., 156, 208
Broadhurst, P. L., 112n
Brobeck, J. R., 46

214

Subject Index

The motive for a deed usually changes during its performance: at least after the deed has been done, it seems quite different.

HEBBEL